86-1595

D1165614

War and Justice

WAR AND JUSTICE

BY ROBERT L. PHILLIPS

UNIVERSITY OF OKLAHOMA PRESS : NORMAN

By Robert L. Phillips

The Philosophy of War (New York, 1975)
(coauthor) *Northern Ireland: Preconditions for Peaceful Negotiations* (Boston, 1983)
War and Justice (Norman, 1984)

Library of Congress Cataloging in Publication Data

Phillips, Robert L. (Robert Lester), 1938–
    War and justice.

    Bibliography: p. 151
    Includes index.
        1. Just war doctrine.   2. Guerrilla warfare—Moral and ethical
aspects.   3. Deterrence (Strategy)—Moral and ethical aspects.
4. War (International law)   I. Title.
U21.2.P47   1984   341.6'2   84-40278
ISBN 0-8061-1893-8

Publication of this work has been made possible in part by a grant from the Andrew W. Mellon Foundation.

The paper in this book meets the guidelines for permanence and durability of the Committee on Production Guidelines for Book Longevity of the Council on Library Resources, Inc.

Justice without force is a myth, because there are always bad men; force without justice stands convicted of itself. We must therefore put together justice and force, and so dispose things that whatever is just is mighty, and whatever is mighty is just.

PASCAL

In the course of my research I shall endeavor to unite what right permits with what interest prescribes, that justice and utility may not be separated.

ROUSSEAU

Contents

Preface

THIS WORK is a defense of the traditional position on the justified use of force by political states, a doctrine commonly labeled *bellum justum* and subdivided into questions having to do with grounds for initiating combats *(jus ad bellum)* and questions having to do with the correct behavior of combatants in wartime *(jus in bello)*. Although the doctrine of the just war is commonly and correctly associated with the political philosophy of the Middle Ages, it has its origin in the very beginning of Western philosophy. For example, in *The Republic* (which is, after all, a military state) Plato spends considerable time discussing the "rules of war." Interestingly and typically, he is concerned mainly with the deleterious effect of unrestrained violence on *Greek* life, without any indication that such considerations might have a larger extension. There are echoes of this parochial outlook in Aristotle's discussion of natural slavery and warfare. Unfortunately, this trend continued until fairly recently in Western history. Two examples will suffice: In 1139 the church proscribed the crossbow, in line with its usual distaste for ballistic weapons, as "hateful to God and unfit for Christians." There was, however, no objection to using it against the infidel. And as late as the eighteenth century a Thomas Puckle invented a gun with two barrels: one fired round shot to be used against Christians, and the other fired square shot for use strictly against the infidel.

Despite these quaint and amusing lapses, Western philosophy exhibits a clear and concise development in the area of just-war thinking. By the late nineteenth century much of the relevant material from medieval political philosophy had become incorporated into international law and into the rules of the various civilized states for land and sea warfare. This was particularly the case with *jus in bello*. Indeed, so much have the principles of justified war become assimilated into modern Western thinking that an intelligent person, unfamiliar with the growing literature on the subject, might well wonder what the fuss is all about. Is the current furor, he might well ask, simply part of the modish concern for "philosophy and public affairs?" Is this not another case of philosophers talking to each other?

The answer, of course, is no. There are developments in the twentieth century that do appear to call for a re-evaluation of a doctrine which has, I believe, proved adequate in the past. As this work is a defense of the traditional position, I shall not have much to add to the substance of just-war theory but shall argue that, despite the very considerable pressures upon it created by modern history, there is, in the end, no alternative but to think about the problem of war in about the same way as did the philosophers who developed the theory.

Normally, critics of *bellum justum* play on one or other of two related themes. Sometimes they argue that the traditional position will no longer do because the rapid advance of weapons technology has produced arms which are essentially indiscriminate. A favorite candidate is the nuclear bomb, but even lesser agencies of destruction, such as napalm and the machine gun, are sometimes said to make any war immoral, regardless of the cause. So that, while in the past someone contemplating a war might very well have mulled over the justice of his cause and then undertaken its prosecution, now, given these essentially indiscriminate weapons, we can no longer go on in this way. Rather, what we now must consider first is what sorts of weapons are likely to be used if war does break out. In extreme versions it is claimed that since *any* war today risks possible escalation to nuclear level, no war may be justified. This line is curious in a number of ways. One obvious rejoinder is to point out that the critic's position is a version of *bellum justum*. For it is on the grounds of lack of discrimination and proportionality of means that such warfare is said to be wrong, but these are principles central to just-war thinking. A persistent misunderstanding is that *bellum justum* entails that some wars must actually be justified, or, perhaps more mildly, that if no wars can be morally undertaken the doctrine has somehow failed. As we shall see, it is not part of just-war thinking to advocate the actual prosecution of some war or to provide an ad hoc justification of some past conflict. Its only concern is to specify conditions under which wars may be justly initiated and prosecuted. If, for whatever reason, there turn out to be no such conditions, then the conclusion that no war can be morally undertaken is inescapable, but then the generation of such conclusions is precisely what the theory is all about.

I do not want to give the impression that modern weapons do not put pressures and strains upon anyone who believes that modern warfare can be justified, or, more seriously, upon someone who believes, as I do, that since war is probably inevitable it is advisable to attend seriously to the question of how to fight it morally. I shall consequently have much to say about weapons of destruction. For now, it is sufficient to note that modern weapons *alone* cannot be blamed for the peculiar horrors of war in our century, as it is naïve in the extreme to suppose a simple causal connection between the existence of a weapon and its employment. For example, rifles were in existence for over two centuries before their devastating employment in modern warfare.* The real question is: What is it about the political and moral climate which persuades millions of people to assent not only to use these weapons against others but to persevere, usually with high courage, when

---

*The first successful rifle appeared in the late fifteenth century in Germany (Brodie, *From Cross-Bow to H-Bomb*, Chap. 3).

those same weapons are turned against them? What, in short, happened between 1716, when the main problem of European armies was desertion—effectively preventing pursuit and rendering a great many battles mere demonstrations—and 1916, when thousands of British infantrymen *walked* in wave after wave straight into German machine guns on the Somme, resulting in 60,000 casualties in the first day alone? Organizational and technological efficiency alone cannot render this changing face of battle, for people must be *willing* to be so organized and to accept weapons of great destructive power.

A criticism closely related to the destructive weapons thesis is the claim that novel forms of warfare render the traditional position irrelevant. A standard example here is guerrilla warfare. The guerrilla or partisan is necessarily in violation of the rules of war: he does not wear a uniform, he slips in and out of the civil population, and he employs random terror. It is true that, although guerrilla war is not novel, it does seriously challenge any attempt to make it a form of morally acceptable conflict. I shall spend a good deal of time discussing these special challenges. At this stage I shall only repeat the point made in connection with novel forms of weaponry: if some *type* of warfare, novel or revived, fails to meet the test of a just war, this by itself represents no defect in the theory.

Perhaps what is more commonly intended by criticisms involving reference to novel weapons and conditions is less to charge just-war theory with falsity or confusion as with otherworldliness. That is, if it is inevitable that such weapons and forms of war be used, then just-war theorists, with their prohibitions and restraints, are simply talking to themselves. They may be right, but they are irrelevant. This is a serious and important argument, and I shall devote much attention to it.

Finally, a brief remark about a matter that is quite beyond the scope of this thesis. The special moral difficulties of fighting wars, conventional or otherwise, in this century arise not primarily out of weapons technology or new de-

partures in combat techniques. These are merely expres-
sions of a deeper root cause, which is, in my opinion,
popular sovereignty. Doctrines of popular sovereignty of
one variety or another inform to a greater or lesser extent
the political systems of the modern world. One practical
effect of this has been to diffuse responsibility for political
acts, including war, over even larger areas. The clearest
outward symbol of this is the conscript army (as opposed
to the impressed army—a distinction perhaps not always
apparent to the conscript, but real all the same; I shall
expand upon this later). Conscription, reintroduced into
Europe at the time of the French Revolution, has now become a permanent part of world political machinery. It has
been a very long time since the initiation and conduct of
war were the province of a special class of political leaders
and their agents. War is still the business of the sovereign,
but if the people *constitute* the sovereign, then acts of war
obviously become the people's business. As we shall see,
one of the great ironies of history is the huge increase in
the scope of wars fought by states animated by theories of
popular sovereignty.

As Robert Leckie puts it:

Conscription, then, actually was the handmaiden of the new
religion of Democracy. Faith in Man was supplanting faith in
God. The mass-man enrolled in mass-armies was now prepared
to make a slaughter which would make previous warfare seem
truly scented indeed. Promising political freedom and equality
for every man, Democracy also compelled every man to fight for
its propagation or defense. The old coin of celestial paradise was
replaced by the new one of terrestrial perfection. But if the new
coin's obverse side proclaimed One Man and One Ballot, its
darker, inverse side said One Man and One Bullet.

Thus, the Democratization of war—the device of the draft by
which mass armies might be raised and inflamed with the spirit
of nationalism—was the single great step by which modern warfare became so terrible and total. True enough, the ensuing
seventeen decades were to witness five more revolutions in Modern War, each making it more devastating; but all of these were

mere differences in degree. The Democratic Revolution was a difference in *kind*.[1]

The widespread belief of Enlightenment advocates of this position was that increased identification of the people with the state would see the gradual disappearance of war. This appeared to be entirely self-evident to philosophers such as Kant, who pointed out in *Perpetual Peace* that it is, after all, the people who contribute the most and lose the most in war. Given systems in which their will prevailed, they would, therefore, always opt for peace. Variations on this theme have been played by utilitarians, socialists, and others. In fact, the "people" have tended to get the worst of all possible worlds. Because of the demand for secrecy, the nature of war itself, and the harsh realities of political bureaucracies, the people are never consulted in the manner these early theorists envisioned; and yet, they are expected to turn out en masse in defenses of the state, in conformity with the doctrine of popular sovereignty. It is also important to note that these Enlightenment philosophers and their followers were, to a man, bitter opponents of *bellum justum*, regarding it as an aristocratic device to prolong the reign of warfare. Whether the traditional doctrine of justice in and of war can survive in a world animated by such political theory is one of the most serious challenges to be faced in this work.

The plan of this work is very simple. I begin with an explication of the doctrine of the just war and a discussion of its particular problems in connection with nuclear weapons and insurgency. I will then discuss and criticize two alternative standpoints: pacifism and realpolitik. I conclude with a short survey of the major issues and a suggestion about the future of warfare.

I wish to thank the following persons who have read this work and made helpful comments on it: A. Montefiorie, J. Glover, and R. M. Hare, all of Oxford University; and J. Kupperman, of the University of Connecticut.

The ethical theory upon which this work is based derives from the Aristotle-Aquinas tradition. In understanding this tradition and its relevance to contemporary problems, I have been greatly assisted by the writings of John Finnis. I am particularly indebted to his *Natural Law and Natural Rights.*

ROBERT L. PHILLIPS

Amston, Connecticut

War and Justice

Introduction

Bellum Justum

THE CONTEMPORARY DOCTRINE of the just war intends to stand as the moral and prudential alternative to absolute pacifism on the one hand and realpolitik or state necessity on the other. Just-war thinkers do not deny the necessities of states to act in their interests and the right of states to use force in the pursuit of those interests. But they will argue that there are, for reasons which will become clear subsequently, inherent or built-in restraints on the use of force. These restraints are, of course, moral and prudential, not natural. They are inherent, it is argued, because war may be rationally undertaken only as a means of achieving a political end and morally undertaken only as a means of distributing justice. These twin purposes rule out an unrestrained use of force as imprudent and immoral. At this level of generality, the theory is purely formal. It claims that if force be used, it must be *justified* and that it cannot be directed at any and every target nor employed in any quantity.

The premise that states have their necessities but are also inherently restrained in the pursuit of those interests appears to perceptive critics as a self-contradiction that allows them to dispose of the theory at the outset. Robert Tucker, in his classic critical study of just-war theory, puts it this way:

Now as in the past, the doctrine of *bellum justum* does not attempt to deal with the critical issue of means simply by abandoning statecraft. In most of its contemporary versions, as in its traditional versions, it seeks instead to square the circle by acknowledging that the state has its necessities and at the same

3

time by insisting that the measures by which these necessities
may be preserved must remain limited.[1]

An important premise of Tucker's criticism is that states,
unlike individuals living within a civil society, are judges in
their own case and that therefore to deprive them of the
right to do whatever they deem necessary is to deprive
them of their sovereignty. Unfortunately, Tucker goes on
to cloud the argument by pointing at length to the somewhat obvious fact that, historically, states have interpreted
the principles of justice in war in such an elastic way that
they have caused them to seem compatible with absolutely
any act of war. It does seem to me, however, to be no very
severe criticism of a moral position that it can be misused.
In any case, the argument that *bellum justum* can with sufficient ingenuity, or incompetence, be bent is different from
the argument that moral principle and state necessity are
incompatible. This latter claim is important and powerful,
and though it obviously has general ramifications through
the whole of political theory, it receives a kind of special
focus in connection with war. In what follows, I shall try
to develop basically three lines of response to this charge
of incompatibility, and I will do this in the course of delineating the doctrine of justice in war.

The first line of response is theological. *Bellum justum*
in its traditional form is one important aspect of medieval
political theory which receives its clearest expression in
the Augustinian contrast between the City of God and the
City of Man. In that context statecraft will always be seen
as an essentially imperfect means for the distribution of
justice. The state will have its necessities, but they will
be subordinate to a higher law. The plausibility of such a
theory will depend upon the credibility of some version of
natural law doctrine. I will do no more than state this position, and it will not form any part of my defense of *bellum
justum*. It will, of course, be an important line of argument
for readers disposed to accept its theological underpinnings.

The second line will depend upon two premises: *(a)* If anything at all can be said to be morally wrong, it is to make a direct attack upon another person with the *intention* of killing him or of doing him an injury for the sake of doing him an injury; and *(b)* pacifism is a morally untenable doctrine. Legitimate civil authority is, therefore, justified in its use of force only to the extent that such use can be shown not to violate *(a)*. A central problem here will be to clarify the moral relevance of intention in the act of killing.

The third line of argument is essentially a version of Plato's argument in *The Republic* to the effect that justice and interest are compatible, that, in fact, justice pays. I shall try to show that any theory of statecraft which fails to be guided by the principles of *bellum justum* is, moral questions aside, imprudent. On my argument the view known as realpolitik turns out to be "unrealistic."

I want now to indulge in a very brief historical survey of the medieval origins of *bellum justum,* primarily to provide some philosophical and theological background for a number of concepts central to the theory.

It is a well-known historical fact that the early Christians leaned toward pacifism.[2] Their refusal to bear arms was not, however, principled in quite the way modern pacifists defend their refusal to use force:

> Whence, then, did Christian pacifism arise? Probably from the Sermon on the Mount, which blessed the poor in spirit, the meek, the merciful and the peacemakers. Early Christianity placed a pacifist interpretation on the Sermon, and so distinguished a saint and churchman as Martain of Tours won a discharge from the Roman Army because of his refusal to kill. One of my favorite saints is Maximilian, a Roman youth of about twenty-one, the son of a soldier, who refused to serve in the army with the statement: "I cannot enlist for I am a Christian." For this admirable, though I think misguided stand, Maximilian lost his head.[3]

Christian pacifism appears to be merely one aspect of a

total disengagement from statecraft and from the "things of this world" generally. Christian pacifists certainly did oppose violence, and much was made of Jesus' admonition to turn the other cheek, but there is no indication that they were using pacifism as a moral tool to effect nonviolent political change. Rather, their opposition to violence and their commitment to the teachings of Jesus entailed the incompatibility of Christianity with statecraft. The Roman persecution of them was clearly based upon this and not upon religion per se, for the Romans were normally willing to admit anyone's deity to the pantheon. It was not that the voice of God took precedence over the voice of Rome but that, given the Christian understanding of Jesus' teachings, a Christian could simply not be a citizen also. For example, the Christians did not morally disapprove of *pagans* becoming soldiers, but a Christian who did so was automatically excommunicated. When these facts are coupled with the prevailing belief among Christians of that day that the return of Jesus was reasonably imminent,* resulting in the destruction of all temporal civil orders, one has the feeling that the moral admonitions against violence expressed by Jesus are inextricably mixed with *passivity* — a serene waiting in faith for the end of the world.

Another well-known historical fact is that the world did not come to an end. Two possibilities were now, in principle at least, open to Christians. They could continue to live in isolated communities within society. There is some evidence that this solution was widely acceptable to the Christian community. Whether any civil society could actually allow such detached communities is, of course, a moot question; the Romans certainly did not appear to be so disposed.

The second possibility was for Christians to abandon strict pacifism and to embrace statecraft without at the

---

*Saint Paul, for example, refers to the "present order of things as passing away" and to the brethren "whose lot has been cast in the closing hours of the world."

same time abandoning Christianity. Christians were in any event doing just that in practice. The problem lay in finding some form of theoretical justification. The main figure here is Augustine with his central distinction between the Two Cities. Given the fact that the Second Coming is postponed, then what is the meaning of civil society for the Christian? The Roman empire, argues Augustine, was created by God so that his people might more effectively convert the world to Christianity. It is no accident that the Romans built excellent roads throughout the known world; this was part of the divine plan to speed missionaries on their way. It was no accident that Roman arms prevailed over other nations; this was God's way of bringing all the peoples of the world together under one civil order better to effect their conversion. And so on.

Having established to his satisfaction that God intended the civil order to be used by Christians in the interim, Augustine now faced the problem of how to square that with the teachings of Jesus and, in particular, how to deal with what appear to be strict prohibitions against using the kind of force which is a necessary feature of statecraft. The arguments with which Augustine attempted to provide this justification are surely among the wonders of Western philosophy. He produces three main lines of argumentation the first two of which are quite implausible, the third slightly plausible.[4]

First, and predictably, Augustine makes much of the glory tales in the Old Testament, and he shows with elaborate scholarship that God frequently ordered undesirables killed, himself took sides in war, and was in general "the God of battle." That the teachings of Jesus are at odds with this scenario appears to trouble Augustine not at all. Jesus was, after all, supposed to be the latest word on ethical matters, but Augustine is prepared to divine the true will of God on the matter of force from other sources.

Augustine, in his second argument, reinforces the deliverances of the first by going on to examine the actual teachings of Jesus. These, he says, are not to be taken as literal prescriptions for Christian practice in this world. They were satisfactory as long as it was thought that the world was ending shortly. In this sense the early church fathers were not wrong in taking these teachings as ethical maxims; they were simply mistaken as to the date of the Second Coming. The continuation of history means that the teachings of Jesus are to be understood as counsels of perfection, as a collection of essences which the phenomenology of the world is ever approaching. They are not guides for conduct in the sense that all are obligated to follow them; rather, taken together, they represent a kind of profile of what a perfect person such as Jesus would be like. As evidence of the essentially symbolic nature of these teachings, Augustine examines the famous injunction to "turn the other cheek." If Jesus had intended this literally, he would not have said "If a man hit you on the right cheek turn the left to him also," for this would make no sense in a world where the vast majority of people are right-handed! The reasoning here is that a right-handed person would land a blow on his opponent's *left* cheek (Augustine seems not to have heard of backhanders).

In addition to counsels of perfection, Augustine says, we may also understand the teachings of Jesus as evangelical counsels. What this third argument means is again that Jesus' remarks are not intended as general prescriptions. Frequently, argues Augustine, Jesus addresses remarks to specific individuals, remarks which meet their special requirements. Thus, for example, the admonition to sell all one's goods and give them to the poor is not directed at mankind generally but specifically at the rich young man (whose wealth was his chief stumbling block with respect to faith) and, by implication, to anyone in similar circumstances.

The upshot of all this is that the *ethical* teachings of Christianity are essentially the Ten Commandments and not the sayings of Jesus, and while the Commandments prohibit murder, they do not forbid or rule out the use of force or, presumably, killing incidental to such acts of force.

One shocked response to all this might be that Augustine
has twisted the teachings of Jesus out of all recognition,
but it does seem to me that the fault lies, partly at least,
with Jesus himself (or his biographers). Augustine is not the
first philosopher to have difficulty in extracting a single,
coherent body of ethical teachings from the sayings of Jesus.
Having said that, however, it does seem reasonably clear
to me that Jesus was a pacifist and that his teachings en-
join others to do likewise. That this was the settled view
of the early Christians, nearest the source, is of crucial
importance. As indicated above, Christian pacifism had a
rather different departure from contemporary pacifism,
but it was pacifism nonetheless and therefore quite incompatible with Augustine's interpretations.

Augustine's understanding of scripture implied permission for a Christian to employ force in a just cause. It was
left to subsequent philosophers, mainly Aquinas, to elaborate and develop the Christian position. Once the hurdle of
pacifism had been surmounted, *bellum justum* developed
almost naturally within the framework of medieval political philosophy. There were, moreover, two forces working
in favor of *bellum justum* as an actual feature of statecraft.

1. The hegemony of Christianity during this period
meant that the church could take a number of specific
steps toward restraining combats. In general, the church
apparently wanted to socialize fighting and bring it under
religious control. War in this view comes to be seen, not
as in classical times, as a test of a man's courage and the
exercise of virtue, but as a trial of strength in which the
God is the referee. War becomes a highly formalized means
of settling disputes, a means crowded about with restrictions, often of great detail. The following examples will
perhaps give the flavor of the time. The church waged a
long and generally successful campaign against ballistic
weapons such as the bow and the slingshot. As one writer
put it, "The arrow knoweth not whither it goes." In other
words, if one releases a shower of arrows or stones, it is

difficult to discriminate targets, and thus it is morally preferable to use only those weapons which can be wielded at close range where the target is visible, such as the sword or lance. In addition to restrictions upon weaponry, certain sorts of people were exempt from attack, such as women, children, the clergy, ambassadors, travelers, pilgrims, the aged, and many other categories. Additionally, the church declared the truce of God, a period variously running from Thursday night to Monday morning, in which no fighting was allowed. Fighting was also prohibited on church property, which was considerable, and those with unresolved differences were urged to settle them at the tournament, that most ritualized combat of all. In short, every effort was made to control fighting with respect to time, place, weapons, purpose, and target.

2. From the Battle of Adrianopole (378) to the Battle of Laupen (1339) the primary mode of warfare was heavy cavalry. The companion of this arm was the medieval code of chivalry. But heavy cavalry was extremely costly. The need for several horses, plus armor for the knight (and later for the horse as well), not to mention pages, grooms, and other hangers-on, meant that only a handful of the more wealthy could afford the cost of combat. Of necessity, then, the art of war came to be practiced mainly by the nobility sworn to a code of honor devised by the church. That in itself tended to limit the scope of combats. The "necessity" is, of course, political, not military.

The economic factor had another restraining effect. No single prince could pay the price for a standing army out of his own revenues. The solution arrived at was for the prince to subdivide his land among other gentry in exchange for forty days' service per year. This continual division and subdivision of European real estate made any kind of centralized political authority virtually impossible — there were simply too many principalities with their private interests to allow war on a large scale or for any extended period of time. Clearly these purely political arrangements militated against an expansion of combats.

Given this social and economic system, the warrior class formed a closed shop: everything possible was done to preserve the status quo. Thus the aristocracy was in accord with church doctrine on weaponry. Heavy cavalry was extremely vulnerable to arrow and the sling, and since these weapons were easy to use and to manufacture, it was in the interest of the aristocracy to prevent their employment by the peasants. In general the aristocracy also found the many other moral restraints on fighting very much in their own interest.

Thus the historical context which saw the full bloom of *bellum justum* was one of almost perfect accord between prudence and morality, at least prudence as perceived by the ruling order. And there, of course, lies the problem. One of the most serious criticisms to be raised against *bellum justum* is that it is precisely an instrument devised to protect some favored form of warfare from encroachment by the unorthodox. We shall see this view advanced by various guerrilla warriors.

The prohibitions and restraints promulgated by the church largely passed into the practices of nations as Europe moved into the modern era. This was particularly the case with those principles coming under *jus in bello*. The decline of Catholic hegemony, however, meant a decline in the moral concensus that supported *bellum justum;* the practices continued, as practices often will, but with increasing confusion and skepticism as to rationale. Moreover, whereas Christian political theory and practice had aimed primarily at stability and order, postmedieval thinkers (of which Machiavelli is first and still unsurpassed) championed progress and expansion. All too often war was the engine of this progress, and states found ready justification for the use of force in the view that the destiny of princes was glory.

From the decline of the Middle Ages until the present, the doctrine of the just war has had a tortured and shadowy history. While remaining a part of official church doctrine, its main provisions have tended to become reduced to practices or observances, without much thought being given to changing conditions or to the kind of political theory needed to support the moral justification of force. The wars of our century now raise, in the most acute form, the question of the relevance and meaning of this traditional position on war. Not only have conventional wars increased in scope and ferocity, but we are faced with the distinct possibility of utterly unrestrained forms of warfare becoming accepted practice.

I outline below, in point form, the doctrine of the just war, and in the following chapters I shall expand upon the points listed without defending them as such. My aim here is merely to make clear what the position is. I shall then consider a series of challenges to it from several points of view, and in the course of that, I shall construct the advertised defense.

BELLUM JUSTUM

Jus ad Bellum

I. Last resort.
II. Declared by legitimate authority.
III. Morally justifiable:
    A. Defense against aggression.
    B. Correction of an injustice that has gone uncorrected by legitimate authority "in another place."
    C. Reestablishment of a social order which will distribute justice.
    D. Undertaken with the intention of bringing about peace.

Jus in Bello

I. Proportionality: The quantity of force employed or threatened must always be morally proportionate to the end being sought in war.

II. Discrimination: Force must never be applied in such a way as to make noncombatants and innocent persons the intentional objects of attack. The only appropriate targets in war are combatants.

  A. The Principle of Double Effect: In a situation where the use of force can be foreseen to have actual or probable multiple effects, some of which are evil, culpability does not attach to the agent if the following conditions are met:

    1. The action must carry the intention to produce morally good consequences.
    2. The evil effects are not *intended* as ends in themselves or as means to other ends, good or evil.
    3. The permission of collateral evil must be justified by considerations of proportionate moral weight.

Chapter 1

Jus ad Bellum

LET us now consider in order the points of the introductory outline. The first thing to note is that the standard translation of *bellum justum* as "just war" may be misleading if it is supposed that war can somehow be itself endowed with moral substance. On the traditional view, war is always an evil insofar as it involves a physical attack upon another person. There may, however, be situations where fighting is the lesser of evils, but in such cases the use of force must be *justified*. Prima facie, attacking another person is evil and, indeed, can never be anything else qua attack. But we may upon occasion find that it is the only means of avoiding an even greater evil. Thus, it may be less misleading to speak of "justified war" instead of "just war."

I. *Last resort*. The foregoing is relevant to the first consideration in the outline. Although war may be sometimes justified, it will always be morally correct to effect it only after it is clear that other means are not adequate to resolve the issue. It is a mistake to suppose that "last" necessarily designates the final move in a chronological series of actions. It *may* do so, as when a policeman pursuing a suspect goes through the steps of challenging the fleeing suspect verbally, then firing a warning shot if that fails, and finally firing at him as a last resort. There may also be cases, however, where time does not permit actually attempting less coercive means. If terrorists are holding some hostages and announce that they will kill them all in two minutes, we would certainly be justified in using force as our first

14

act (Entebbe-style), though it would still be as a last resort. We have to understand that there is a suppressed hypothetical in this restraint, namely, if time and other relevant conditions permit, other means short of force ought to be tried, but we are not to be locked into a series of steps beginning with the most pacific means and gradually escalating in the direction of force. If we could ideally arrange matters of fact, that would be the scenario, but failing that, sometimes force will be our first step.

Clearly, the criteria for making such a decision to activate force rather than some other means are not to be found in *bellum justum* itself. The doctrine presupposes and is parasitic upon there already being moral principles (and rationality). This may be the place to make the point that the doctrine is not itself a collection of moral principles but is, rather, a series of questions which any moral agent must ask himself when faced with the problem of resort to force. The doctrine of justified war *by itself* does not provide adequate moral guidance. In particular, *bellum justum* also constitutes an effort to make statecraft compatible with the moral principle forbidding murder, as well as sundry other prohibitions against doing violence to others. Unless these have been accepted or internalized as one's own moral principles, the doctrine will not make much sense. This is crucial, because critics often fail to understand that *bellum justum* is essentially a moral tool or device whose purpose is to allow us to sort out or anatomize a situation to which two prima facie conflicting sets of principles are said to apply, namely, principles of statecraft and morality. So the last-resort provision, for example, reflects the seriousness with which moral agents regard acts of force directed against other human beings and thus presupposes "the moral point of view." Of course, if one does not take the perspective on things, *bellum justum* will appear to beg the question. I do have an important line of argument which says that, in this area at least, morality and prudence are identical, but that is a separate argument. At this point, *bellum justum* is intelligible only in conjunction with moral prohibitions against murder and acts of violence directed against others.

II.   *Declared by legitimate authority.*   The claim that war must be declared by legitimate authority only is in some ways ambiguous. Part of the intent of this provision was to rule out private warfare, partly because the prince was conceived, in medieval political philosophy, as the pipeline of divine will; and partly because it was feared that private war would degenerate into mere revenge. Also, once private war becomes established practice, it is difficult to restrain the spread of violence, as people will tend to resort to it as they please and for trivial reasons. So while an individual may well have received an injury which would justify resort to force, *he* must not effect it. These considerations suggest that the use of force by legitimate authority is a matter of caution and does not involve the claim that only states are injured (that is, that individuals are not the objects of attack). It is possible, I suppose, to argue that an attack upon the subject is an attack upon the sovereign, but generally speaking this restraint has been interpreted as prohibiting private warfare because of likely undesirable consequences of *not* doing so.

One can certainly *imagine* circumstances where some social unit other than the state might be morally justified in going to war. Suppose, for example, a province of a decadent empire is under attack by an aggresor whose intent is to exterminate the inhabitants of the province. The refusal of legitimate imperial authority to defend them would surely not obligate the provincials to surrender. So at least one criterion of legitimacy seems to be the willingness of authority to protect those for whom it has political responsibility. It is in this sense, I think, that the various formulations of social contract theory (Hobbes, Locke, and Rousseau) embody an important truth about political life.

The legitimate-authority principle seems reasonable enough. It is difficult to imagine a political system failing to subscribe to it, if only for prudential reasons. It might even be said to be entailed by civil society, or to be part of the definition of civil society. The difficulty here is, therefore, not with the correctness of the restraint, given a world composed of political states, but over the question: Who, or what, *is* legitimate authority? The claim that war may only be undertaken by legitimate authority, while perfectly correct, may involve question-begging where the issue which provoked fighting is precisely a dispute about who is the bearer of that authority. One of the more poignant instances of this problem was the American claim, reiterated endlessly over twelve years, that United States forces were in Vietnam at the invitation of the legitimate government. As it became progressively clearer that legitimacy was the main issue of the war, the American position rang all the more hollow.

The problem of legitimacy will wax or wane depending upon the predominant political philosophies of the day. Hereditary monarchy, that most successful of all political systems, will probably have an easier time of it, since all that matters is correct blood; but even here there will be rival claimants with more or better blood than others. States depending upon some theory of the "general will" will probably have the worst time of it, and the rest will be strung out between. The paradox is, of course, that war itself is most frequently the means whereby questions of legitimacy are decided in the eyes of the community of nations (though rival claimants may not accept this verdict). Thus in the context of a civil war the principle runs into problems. Here again we are faced with a situation where *bellum justum* ramifies into larger issues in political philosophy, particularly with those concerning de facto and de jure authority. These questions cannot really be satisfactorily explored in the confines of this work. What can be said here is this: The claim that war may be undertaken only by legitimate authority reflects a political reality, namely, that factions at war *will* seek to establish their legitimacy. No matter how divided they may be on other issues, they both seek to be recognized as legitimate by their own people and by the community of nations. Thus they will both agree that the authority to use force is decided by legitimacy. What the principle does in these difficult cases is not, obviously, to tell us which among the contending factions is sovereign but to focus our attention on the centrality of the connection between legitimacy and permission to use force. It emphasizes, that is to say, that for the community of nations political power is not simply there for the taking by force at any time that anyone so chooses but that justified force is inextricably tied to a decision about legitimate authority. Our attention is thereby turned from questions of simple power to gain control and toward the issue of the right to govern. That is, one rarely (if ever) finds states basing their claims to use force on force *alone*.

III. *Morally justifiable.* (A) The right to self-defense against an aggressor has always been regarded as fundamental by most just-war advocates. There have been some curious exceptions. Augustine, for example, says that if he were crossing a desert and found himself set upon by a murderer he would probably follow Jesus' counsel of perfection and turn the other cheek, but if he saw the same brigand attacking a helpless woman, he would intervene, for *that* would be an act of charity and not merely an attempt to save his own life. Augustine's point seems to be that killing another person to save one's own life is a supreme act of selfishness. Augustine seems to be alone in this eccentric analysis of self-defense, for the bulk of just-war thinking suggests that, while the death of any person is an evil, an aggressor who refuses to stop what he is doing is responsible for his own death. What a person does not have a right to do is intend the death of the aggressor, in the sense that the purpose of his action should be to stop the aggressor from doing what he is doing. The aggressor's death may thus be accepted or justified as a collateral event if the only means of stopping him is killing. This claim is fraught with difficulties that I will tackle in due course.

The essence of just-war thinking on this point is that if there is a moral obligation to refrain from making direct attacks upon others then one has a right not to have these attacks directed at oneself. Something more must obviously be said here, however, for this assertion is one with which a pacifist will concur. What must be added is that a person also has the right to use force to prevent the abrogation of his right not to have violence done to him; otherwise, "having" the right is a sham. There is no sense in which one can be said to have a right if one must always acquiesce in its removal. The *level* of force that one may use in the defense of this right is limited in various ways—one is not justified in using an atomic bomb in response to a snowball attack. These limitations are covered in the next chapter, which concerns *jus in bello.*

A state, like an individual, also has the right of defense against aggression. This has not generally been taken to mean that a state must always wait until it is attacked before using force. Just as the last-resort provision does not entail a temporal sequence culminating in force, so defense against aggression has not been thought to entail a prior act of force. If a state is morally certain that it is about to be attacked, it may launch a preemptive strike. There are certain sorts of exception to this permission. For example, the killing of children of traditional enemies was a question much debated by early just-war theorists. If one expects war to go on for an indefinite period, then why not kill the children of the enemy, their future warriors? The consensus on this question was that, while a preemptive strike might be justified in face of imminent hostilities, the "killing in anticipation" of children could in no way be sanctioned. Not only are the children innocent, but there is no indication that war will necessarily be prolonged, or at least the evidence is not strong enough to construe children as combatants.

An interesting modification of the right to self-defense has taken place in the twentieth century. According to the current usages of international law, as well as the provisions of the United Nations, preemptive strikes are not permitted as a justified use of armed force. The criterion of aggression is troops-across-borders and not hostile intent. The rationale for this new position is that the consequences of modern war are so serious that nothing short of a direct attack by an aggressor warrants resort to arms. One might think that the very seriousness of modern war would support the doctrine of preemptive strikes as a means, at least under some circumstances, of nipping war in the bud. Contemporary theorists appear to believe however, that the risks of special pleading outweigh any benefits to be accrued by permitting nations to judge that war may be undertaken on the basis of a criterion other than invasion.

(B) The traditional version of *bellum justum* holds that a Christian prince has an obligation to intervene in the affairs of another state if there is an injustice there that continues to be uncorrected by legitimate authority. As with preemptive strikes, this provision has also been dropped from modern international law, as well as from the United Nations, partly because of the "seriousness of modern war" argument and partly because of an almost fanatical concern for absolute national sovereignty in the postcolonial world—Western world, that is. Under current thinking, if the Nazis had not moved beyond the borders of the Reich, they could have murdered any number of Jews and other undesirables without fear of outside intervention. There would, no doubt, be economic boycotts and other such censures, but no armed intervention—no war (as in South Africa, Hungary, Czechoslavakia, and Uganda). Such a position would have been inconceivable before the current era. It should not be supposed that modern thinking is simply infected with moral relativism in its rejection of (B); rather, the argument is based upon a calculation of the lesser of evils. Such is the danger of escalation to nuclear war that the toleration of any amount of localized evil is preferable to running the risk of bringing about the destruction of the world. When one combines that fact with the possibility of special pleading on the part of nations as a means of intervening in the affairs of their neighbors, it is morally preferable to outlaw war altogether as a means of correcting injustice in cases not involving aggression.

It may seem perverse to accept *any* amount of localized evil rather than intervene in the affairs of a sovereign state. After all, is sovereignty all that important? I believe we have to say that states ought not to interfere in the affairs of sovereign states for three reasons: (1) such intrusions risk escalation to nuclear war, (2) they impede the establishment of an international order, and (3) they abrogate the obligation of peoples to sort out their own political and social problems.

We ought to be prepared, however, to override this rule where a state fails to guarantee those minimal rights which justify its existence. For if it consistently fails to protect the "life, liberty, and property" of its inhabitants, one might very well argue that the sovereignty is dissolved anyway and that therefore there *is* no intervention in the affairs of a sovereign state.

(C) If the purpose of political society is the distribution of justice, and if war is a permissible political act, then the purpose of war must ultimately be directed toward reestablishing a just order. This position is formal in the sense that it does not itself specify any particular ideology or social model but is dependent upon such things for its content.

(D) While war may sometimes be justified, it is always morally undesirable as a "state of affairs." Thus the decision to go to war must be accompanied with the intention to effect peace. This rules out various theories which recommend war as therapeutic or as desirable for the glory it brings the sovereign. Another provision which is sometimes attached to (D) holds that war should not be undertaken unless there is a reasonable prospect of winning. This reflects the fact that war is essentially an *agreement* between two states to settle a dispute by arbitrament of arms. A state is not morally justified in resorting to war and subjecting its citizens to death unless there is at least a chance of favorable outcome. Thus, Luxembourg chose to surrender to the Germans in 1940 rather than resist against hopeless odds. This is a curious provision in many ways, particularly when one attempts to balance loss of life in a hopeless struggle against perhaps centuries of slavery. Might not a populace wish to die fighting rather than submit under such circumstances?

The argument that states have the right to defend themselves against acts of aggression seems well founded in moral thinking. Aggression not only threatens the right of people to participate in basic human values but also undermines the "space" in which these values may be actualized.

The problem with the right to self-defense is that aggressors may need to be countered before they come tumbling across one's border. Also, the traditional doctrine of *bellum justum* positively requires that states extend military help to victims of injustice. Thus questions of when and whether a state has the right to intervene in the affairs of another sovereign state, or to strike preemptively, arise frequently and are, of course, extremely difficult to answer. There is no general formula here, obviously, but perhaps there is a starting point. We may say that a state has the right to intervene in the affairs of another (and, a fortiori, to preempt) where there is an overt and systematic program of injustice (Locke's "long train of abuses"). Such a state need not, however, have a positive duty to do so, for any state must first see that its promises, pledges, responsibilities, and commitments to its own people are satisfied before offering their blood and treasure to others. Yet the *right* to correct injustices remains, and any state has the right to enforce the moral law.

This traditional view is challenged by a line of liberal political theory running from John Stuart Mill to Michael Walzer. It says that what we should attempt to achieve internationally is not just or free societies but *self-determining* ones, on the grounds that people have a right to work out their own destinies without outside interference *even if* this requires toleration of considerable local injustice. This view seems to me to be, in principle, wrongheaded, for it denies to strangers the concern and help that one would naturally extend to a friend and, indeed, even in many instances to a stranger. If I were to see a man walking over the edge of a precipice, I should be inclined to tackle him first and reason with him later. Thus one nation might so restrain another, with justice, from some act of self-injury.

It is very important, in combating the liberal position, to undermine, at the outset, their most important claim. Liberals like to construe the debate with traditionalists as one between evenhanded fairness (self-determination) and "paternalism." Their opponents, they claim, are being paternalistic when they intervene to sort out the affairs of others, thus denying them the right to achieve virtue on their own. Now it is certainly true that virtue cannot be merely imposed from the outside. Individuals (or peoples) must interiorize virtue, must make moral rules *their* rules. In spite of this, no one would deny that the *teaching* of virtue is important, and war is certainly an instrument of teaching. Yet the central issue remains the charge of paternalism. The contrast that the liberal wishes to make between fairness and paternalism fails. For the liberal to contend that under the traditional doctrine people are not treated with an even hand is surely to invite the reply: Under a system of liberal self-determination, are people who have strong convictions about their duty to correct injustices being treated with an "even hand"? Is *their* conception of a just international society given "due consideration" under the system of self-determination?

We should be clear that both the liberal and the traditionalist are advancing ideologically charged views; both have visions of what international society ought to look like, visions rooted ultimately in some commitment to basic human values. The liberal typically conceals his commitment by contrasting his position with "paternalism" as value-free.

In this regard it is important to look more closely at the

idea of self-determination. In *Just and Unjust Wars*, Walzer champions a form of self-determination which he takes over from the nineteenth-century utilitarian Henry Sidgwick.[1] According to Sidgwick, what counts in cases of sovereignty disputes between legalistic land-title claims as against the wishes of the people living there is what those people want. Sidgwick argues that in a case where an aggressor unjustly subdues a populace only to find that, over the years, these people come to actually prefer the invader's rule, it would constitute a new aggression for their former sovereign to try to reclaim his lost territories! Granted, the original aggression was unjust, but so would be any effort to restore sovereignty against the people's wishes. Walzer coins a slogan to express this doctrine: "The land follows the people." Now this seems in many ways an attractive doctrine with its concern for people and their wishes over mere legal title. It is also "distributionist" in that it sees human needs taking precedence over property rights. A closer investigation of the doctrine of self-determination, however, reveals problems. Let us approach these by means of an example: Suppose that upon a vacant section of the Florida coastline a boatload of Cuban refugees arrives. They are carrying a banner inscribed "The Land Follows the People." Why is this not a legitimate act of self-determination? I suggest that it is difficult to fault this under most theories of self-determination. Here we have in every sense "a people" arriving upon land "not sufficiently inhabited." Yet no one would regard these people as having a shred of a right to sovereignty. It is obvious that claims to self-determination cut no ice if the claimants have only arrived this morning. Thus "what the people living there want" (simpliciter) cannot possibly be what "finally counts." What seems to be required is some period of occupancy, but for how long is not clear. Occupancy, per se, really has nothing to do with self-determination. If occupancy is what counts, then what need have we for self-determination (as meaning what the people living there want)? Further, if occupancy is what counts, those who claim legal title can often trace longer periods of occupancy (as in Ulster). There is a further puzzle. If some piece of real estate was justly acquired and legally owned, how does occupancy by someone alter that fact? Robert Nozick raises this question by way of the example of rent control. If I own an apartment building which I justly acquired, why does long-term occupancy by my tenants entitle them to a share in my property? To this question there is probably no generally agreed-upon answer because there is no generally agreed-upon answer to the prior question: How does one justly acquire a property in the first place?

Perhaps two different things have been confused here. It is certainly true that if someone is under threat of death he may use property which does not belong to him to save his life. If I am drowning, I certainly have the right to use someone else's boat which I find floating nearby. But this in no way gives me a share in the ownership of the boat. Similarly, my Cuban refugees arguably have a right to land on the beach and to defend themselves against murderous attacks by irate Florida landowners, but they thereby hardly achieve sovereignty.

The vagueness of the concept of self-determination should warn us against any easy solution of the sloganistic sort characteristic of liberal political theory. As a final confirmation of this point we have to consider only three contemporary examples of the appeal to self-determination.

First, Northern Ireland: Here the Ulster Protestants claim that as "a people" they have the right of self-determination, which for them means continued union with Britain. The nationalists, on the other hand, claim that self-determination for the "whole island" would result in the reunification of Ireland. Moreover, nationalists argue that Protestants are merely interlopers, invaders (albeit since 1640) who had no right to be there in the first place.

Second, the Middle East: The Israelis appeal to self-determination and so do the Palestinians (neither cynically). The Arabs perceive the Jews as merely another group of European peoples who from the Crusades onward have sought to extend sovereignty over Arab land.

Third, the Falklands: The British argue that the Falklanders have the right of self-determination in virtue of their desire to remain British, whereas the Argentinians claim sovereignty on the basis of their legal succession to the Spanish empire. The Falklanders are, for them, not an indigenous people but a mere colonial plantation.

What these three examples have in common are various "peoples" proclaiming the right to sovereignty on the basis of self-determination, where their opponents see them as mere squatters on their territory, like my Cuban refugees. I suggest that what is crucial in these cases where war and civil strife have actually occurred is that the doctrine of self-determination is entirely unhelpful. For it is clear that that theory requires some *prior* conception of rights related to occupancy in some original or primitive sense. "What the people living there want is what finally counts" is an effective argument only if such people are clearly perceived to have some "organic" connection with the land, a connection which remains unanalyzed in theories of self-determination.

To summarize *jus ad bellum*: Wars of aggression are permitted under the traditional doctrine only if the cause is just; but all wars of aggression are prohibited under the modern interpretation, for no matter how serious the injury to a state, modern warfare is an immoral means for settling grievances and altering existing conditions. This amendment has been made for two reasons. First, the destructiveness of modern war makes it a wholly disproportionate means for the resolution of international disputes and for the redress of grievances, even where they are just. Second, to admit the right of states to initiate combats, even to correct injustice, would impede efforts of the world community to establish a judicial method of outlawing war altogether.

A war of defense against the injustice of aggression is

morally permissible in both the traditional and the modern view. This is perceived as in no way a contradiction of the concern for peace, for peace may require defense: "The precept of peace is of divine right. Its purpose is to protect the goods of humanity, inasmuch as they are the goods of the Creator. Among these goods there are some of such importance for the human community that their defense against an unjust aggression is without doubt fully justified."[2]

As noted earlier, it is the intention of just-war theory to occupy an intermediate position between the extremes of pacifism and realpolitik. A final defense of *jus ad bellum* will have to wait until our analysis of those two extreme views is completed.

Chapter 2

Jus in Bello

THE "other half" of *bellum justum* is *jus in bello,* or the doctrine of just behavior in combat. We return to the introductory outline:

I. *Proportionality.* The principle of proportionality holds that in cases where the use of force is justified it cannot be employed in absolutely any measure. Obviously, if the aim of war is the correction of injustice, then the level of force must not be such as to create new and greater injustices. This principle is sometimes confused with the doctrine of "minimal force," which holds that the least amount of force consistent with effecting the desired ends ought to be our goal. While minimal force should always be used, we also have to consider the *degree* of violence, for some military tasks might very well require a minimum of force which would be disproportionate. That is, our calculations must include not only a forecast of necessary minimal means but also of consequences.

This distinction is of crucial importance because it directs our attention to the means of waging war and thus to the moral questions provoked by certain types of weaponry. In effect, proportionality is not to be calculated relative to a weapons system taken as a "given" but, rather, in terms of a calculus which will include the weapons themselves. So, for example, it may not be morally acceptable to say the following sort of thing: Given the fact of nuclear weapons deployed for massive retaliation, what casualty level is acceptable within the possibilities of these devices? Now this is precisely what some military thinkers have attempted to do (as we shall see in a later discussion of nuclear warfare), but my contention here is that this move renders the whole conception of proportionality vacuous by making its significance dependent upon whatever weapons happen to exist at a given time. It is, of course, extremely difficult to counter in any meaningful way the onrush of weapons technology. The operative principle of the technocrat is: "If x is possible, then x ought to be"; but the alternative to not doing this is making morality completely subordinate to whatever technological development happens to be occuring at the moment.

I hasten to add that the motivation of those who argue that proportionality is relative to conditions is not simply self-serving. If one knows that certain sorts of weapons will be used which one also knows will cause casualties that are disproportionate on any objective basis, it is obviously morally preferable to attempt to obtain whatever proportionality is possible relative to the system—even in the case of massive retaliation with nuclear weapons. The danger here is that we will fall into the habit of doing no more than this. I suggest that modern history reveals just this pattern of thinking by just-war theorists. A weapon is invented and employed, and suddenly it is a fait accompli. Morality then tags along with a "justification" based ultimately on the principle that even if the means are disproportionate in themselves it is better to try to limit their use than to permit unrestrained employment. This is a principle with which one cannot disagree, but it must not be our guiding principle in thinking about means. Rather, we must evolve some conception of proportion which will allow us to include weapons and modes of warfare *as such* in our prohibitions. It is not, of course, the province of *bellum justum* to provide a criterion of nonrelative proportionality but only to establish that the principles of justice do in fact require such a standard.

II. *Discrimination.*   What is true for proportionality is a fortiori true for the principle of discrimination. The notion that force ought to be morally justified only if it can be employed in a discriminate manner lies at the heart of *jus in bello*. The principle of double effect is, in turn, at the heart of discrimination.

(A) Put as simply as possible, by emphasizing intention as the defining feature of moral actions, the supporters of *bellum justum* attempt to mark a difference between killing in war and murder in two different cases. First, the killing of enemy combatants in a justified war may be morally acceptable under some circumstances. Second, the killing of noncombatants incidental to the prosecution of a necessary military operation in a justified war may also be morally acceptable under some circumstances. I want to spend some time here examining these two cases.

The principle of double effect is a refinement of a more general set of considerations having to do with the discriminating use of force. If the use of force by legitimate authority is to be justified, then obviously it cannot be administered in any quantity nor can it be directed at any and every target. This is "obvious" because we are assuming that if anything can be said to be evil it is direct acts of violence upon other people. If there is to be a distinction between killing in war and murder, there must also be a prior conception of relevant differences in potential targets. The most widely discussed aspect of double effect has been noncombatant immunity, and one of the key issues raised here is how to make such immunity compatible with the foreknowledge which we will normally possess of the certain death of noncombatants incidental to military operations.

Double effect is derived from a quite general criterion of moral judgment enunciated succinctly but clearly by Aquinas: "now moral acts take their species according to what is intended and not according to what is beside the intention, since this is accidental" (*Summa* 2.2, q. 64, art. 7).

Aquinas, I take it, is arguing not that the consequences of actions are morally irrelevant but, rather, that when one raises questions about the morality of a particular action (as opposed to its utility, its beauty, and so on) one is inevitably making reference to the agent's intentions. "Accidental" is used here not exclusively to mean the unforeseen but to include the foreseen but undesired consequences of the action. "Accidental" may be understood as "collateral."

Following this line, we may summarize the principle in the following way: In a situation where the use of force can be seen to have actual or probable multiple effects, some of which are evil, culpability does not attach to the agent if the following conditions are met: (1) the action is intended to produce morally good consequences; (2) the evil effects are not intended as ends in themselves or as means to other ends, good or evil; and (3) the permission of collateral evil must be justified by considerations of proportionate moral weight.

How do these considerations apply to the combat situation? There are at least two senses in which it is sometimes claimed that there is no relevant distinction between killing in war and murder. First is the view that all killing is murder, that it is always wrong deliberately to take another human life. This would mean that in the combat situation it would be wrong to kill both combatants *and* noncombatants and, indeed, that there is really no moral difference between these classes. This is clearly a version of pacifism, a view which I will consider in detail in the next section. For now, however, we can say that this view holds that under no circumstances may the death of another human being be directly willed; killing is wrong even if one's own life is placed in grave risk and even if the other person is the aggressor.

According to the second view, the killing of noncombatants is murder, while the death of an aggressor combatant in wartime is morally acceptable. Thus if a war could be fought entirely between combatants, it would be, in principle, possible to avoid committing murder. It is further argued, however, that in an actual combat situation where there is foreknowledge that operations will cause the death of noncombatants, there is no relevant difference between killing and murder. This view has generated two rather strikingly different conclusions with respect to what a moral agent ought to do faced with the possibility of combat.

On the one hand, since modern weaponry is by its very nature indiscriminate, and since foreknowledge of the death of noncombatants cancels whatever good intentions we may offer by way of exculpation, we end up as pacifists by default. While admitting the theoretical possibility of a just war, the indiscriminate use of force which must necessarily be a feature of contemporary warfare makes us pacifists, as it were, "war by war."

On the other hand, starting from the same premises, it has sometimes been argued that since there are no relevant differences between killing and murder with respect to noncombatants, war may be fought without any restraint at all. That is, if a war is justified then the absence of criteria for distinguishing between killing and murder is a permission to employ any means whatever to bring about victory. This argument is frequently found embedded in a larger utilitarian framework which, in extreme cases, would permit the killing of noncombatants as a means of securing peace. This seems to have been the line taken by Sir Arthur Harris over the British terror bombing of German cities in the Second World War. When reproached with the indiscriminate character of carpet bombing Harris replied, "It is war itself which is evil," thus implying the pointlessness of attempting to make distinctions (at least for the purposes of bombing) between combatants and noncombatants.

These then are the two main lines of criticism directed against the moral significance of the principle of double effect and, consequently, of the distinction between killing in war and murder.

Let us turn first to the question: How can we escape the charge that killing an enemy combatant is murder? If force is ever to be morally justified, its employment must be against a target other than a person as such. One must not be directly seeking the death of another human being either as such or as a means to some further end. Therefore, the intention or purpose of the act of force must be toward *restraint* of the aggressor. This is the beginning of an answer to the pacifist. For he and the defender of *bellum justum* are surely in agreement, and correctly so, that the death of another human being ought never to be directly willed if the target is the man himself in his humanity or the man who represents the values of the enemy in a particular historical situation (this prohibition must imply the intrinsic value of other persons). Yet, if force may be justified, then what is the target? The answer must be that the proper target of the discriminate use of force is not the man himself but the combatant *in* the man.

It may be objected that it is a logical impossibility to separate out the totality of actions plus the underlying rationale for such behavior which together constitute the combatant in the man. That is, to speak of a particular man or of "man" in general apart from particular behavior patterns is to speak of a nonentity. Hence, the combatant in the man is not a possible target. Furthermore, it may be urged that even if some such distinction is possible, to kill one is to kill the other. A soldier going into combat with the intention of restraining or incapacitating combatants must know before he ever lifts a weapon that combat will result in the death of a great many persons.

A utilitarian might put the objection in the following way: Jones and Smith both go into combat armed with machine guns. Jones, a supporter of the traditional view, carries with him the intention to incapacitate or restrain the aggressor, whereas Smith intends merely to kill as many of the enemy as he can in order to avoid being killed himself. On meeting the enemy they both open fire, and they both kill one enemy each. What difference does "intention" make from the moral point of view? In both cases an act of extreme violence, the unleashing of a stream of bullets, has resulted in the death of a person. A corpse lies before both Smith and Jones—this is the brute, ultimate fact which no amount of "intentional" redescription can alter. Thus,

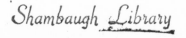

there is only *one* action here, the killing (possibly murder) of a human being.

In trying to answer this there are two things that have to be said about intention. The first has to do with the way in which awareness of an agent's intentions is crucial in understanding the meaning of an action and consequently in knowing how correctly to describe it. If one were to universalize the utilitarian's position on the irrelevance of intention, the results would be quite disastrous for any attempt to understand human action. Setting the moral question entirely aside, we would be unable to make intelligible whole classes of human behavior if we supposed that such behavior could even be described as human action without making intention central. That is, there are cases where two quite different actions are identical with respect to result, observable behavior, and foreknowledge of the result; and the *only* way to distinguish the two is by reference to intention. As an example, take the case of self-killing. If we follow the critic's suggestion and consider as relevant only foreknowledge of result, behavior patterns, and end result (a corpse), then suicide would be effectively defined as *any* action which the agent knew would bring about his own death. This is clearly absurd, for it would not permit us to distinguish between an officer who shoots himself in order to avoid a court-martial and an officer of the same regiment who courageously fights a rear-guard action in such a way that he knows he will not survive. In both cases there is foreknowledge of one's own death, there are objective behavior patterns leading to that result, and there is the result itself. They differ importantly only with respect to intention. Intention is what makes them different actions. To put the point in a general way, failure to take account of intention means that we are unable to make the difference between doing x in order that y shall result and doing x knowing that y will result.[1]

Smith and Jones both have foreknowledge of the impending death of the enemy, they both take identical action, and the result is the same — the enemy soldier is dead.

And yet there are two different actions here: Jones does *x* knowing that *y* will result; Smith does *x* in order that *y* shall result. Well, the critic might reply, there certainly is a difference in intention here, and, thus a description of what is happening will have to make reference to all the facts. Granted, if we want to understand thoroughly what is going on here, then we must take account not only of what the agent knows and foreknows, of behavior and results, but also of what the agent supposes himself to be doing; and that will involve us in including the element of intention in our explanation of his behavior. Having granted this, one has not shown that intention makes any *moral* difference.

The critic is correct. What has been established so far is that intention is a criterion for distinguishing *different* human actions. The importance of this is that in order to show that different moral verdicts are to be applied to Smith and Jones, we first have to show that there were two separate actions involved. The *moral* difference between their actions is, of course, a different matter. What is the difference? Let us recall the objection: The critic will say that it is sophistry to suppose any moral significance in directing force toward the restraint or incapacitation of the combatant while at the same time using means which we know will result in his death. The end result is the same and will be foreknown to be the same, whether or not we "directly" attack the man.

The crucial difference between Smith and Jones is that the latter is logically committed to behaving differently toward those enemy soldiers who have removed themselves from the role of combatant than is his companion Smith. The belief that force must be directed against the combatant and not against the man is the only presupposition which could provide a moral basis for taking prisoners. Smith would have no reason to observe this distinction. He might, on a whim or for immediate prudential reasons, decide to spare the life of the enemy, but he is not logically committed by his beliefs to doing so. The almost universal belief that a man who voluntarily restrains himself or who is restrained by being wounded ought to be immune from attack is only intelligible on the basis of the distinction between the man and the combatant in the man. The moral principle that prisoners ought to be taken and well treated will itself be justified by showing that it is impossible, except in some wholly imprudent fashion, to universalize the killing of those who have surrendered. That is, no rational being could consistently will the killing of all prisoners and include himself in his own prescription. Thus while Jones will have foreknowledge of the death of the aggressor (an admitted evil) the thrust of his actions will be against the combatant and not the man, and the moral payoff of this is that only he is logically committed to observe the moral principle concerning prisoner immunity. To summarize: To those who argue that there is no relevant difference between killing in war and murder in the case of one combatant killing another, we may reply that it is possible, given a well-thought-out doctrine for the justification of the use of force, to direct forceful actions in such a way that while the death of the enemy may be foreknown it is not willed. The purpose of combats as expressed in the actions of individual soldiers is the incapacitation or restraint of an enemy combatant from doing what he is doing as a soldier in a particular historical situation; it is not the killing of a man. This is the essence of the distinction between killing in war and murder in the case of combatants, and the moral relevance of the premise is exhibited in the obligation to acknowledge prisoner immunity, an obligation not incumbent upon someone who fails to observe the central distinction between the man and the combatant in the man.[2]

Before going on to explore more deeply the concept of intention, I want to make two points about the issue of prisoner immunity, for it is crucial to an understanding of my defense of justified killing.

First, I have said that the moral argument against killing prisoners is the impossibility of rational beings to universalize such a procedure. That is, one could *verbally* universalize such a procedure but only on the basis of a departure from rationality or under some type of external duress. Neither of these cases would be based on a moral principle. Now it has been argued that the ill treatment of Allied prisoners by the Japanese in World War II is a counterexample, because their practices derived from consistent moral principles. The Japanese, it is said, believed that once a person became a soldier and took the oath to die for the emperor there was no way he could divest himself of what we have called the combatant in the man. Thus no Japanese soldier must be permitted to surrender or to allow himself to be captured. A person who does so is effectively dead—such is the disgrace. If a soldier may not give up the combatant status in his own case, then it would appear to follow that there is no moral obligation either to take prisoners in the first place or, having taken them for whatever reason, to treat them as anything but slaves. So the Japanese were not simply being gratuitously cruel when they tortured, starved, and otherwise mistreated Allied prisoners; they were acting on principle and were prepared to include themselves in their own prescriptions for others.

One way of dealing with this Japanese example would be to argue that, while they were indeed being consistent, the maxim guiding their actions could be universalized only irrationally. Indeed, this seems to me to be quite clearly the case. I have been unable to discover any remotely rational justification for the use of force which would entail the killing of surrendered combatants or their reduction to slavery *on principle*. But critics might regard this reply as tendentious, that is, there are different concepts of "rationality," or "rationality" is itself an evaluative term, and so on. Thus, for us to impose *our* concept of what would be reasonable upon the Japanese is ethnocentric. This line of thinking strikes me as placing an undue emphasis on purely cultural and historical differences between people, but there is, in any event, an easier way to deal with this Japanese example which avoids these objections altogether.

In the first place, the Code of Bushido to which the Japanese military have for centuries subscribed explicitly requires the correct treatment of prisoners.[3] After General Jonathan Wainwright surrendered the Philippines to Japanese forces, there was a very definite split in the Japanese high command about what was to be done. There was considerable confusion over the whole issue, some appealing to Bushido, some wishing to construe Allied prisoners as capital criminals, and some wishing to reject the whole possibility of prisoner immunity. The point is that there was no single Japanese position on this issue, and thus there was often wide variation in how prisoners were treated. Local commanders, often at a quite low level, would simply decide in an ad hoc fashion what was to be done. Where there was cruelty, it appears to have been the result of certain behavior patterns instilled into recruits in the course of their training, rather than moral principle.

Furthermore, in his brilliant study of the Pacific war John Tolland notes that the practice of superiors beating and slapping subordinates was a pervasive feature of Japanese life: husbands beat wives, older children beat younger ones, teachers beat students, police beat civilians. In the army this was continued and amplified, and it is Tolland's point that the ill treatment or killing of prisoners was simply the logical extension of traditional methods of discipline.

As for the Japanese themselves never surrendering, millions of them obviously did. The question is whether there was some kind of recognizable moral principle or argument at work in the case of those who refused to give up. Once again, the principal motivation appears to have been fear of social consequences instilled into a people traditionally subservient to authority by the Japanese high command as a means of ensuring that the army would fight fanatically. For example, if a soldier was taken prisoner even while he was wounded or unconscious, he was considered officially dead, and his name was removed from the village or ward register. *The Soldier's Manual,* which was issued to the entire army, put it this way: "Bear in mind the fact that to be captured means not only disgracing the army, but your parents and family will never be able to hold up their heads again. Always save the last round for yourself."[4]

To reinforce all this, the Japanese were told that if they did surrender they would be tortured to death by the Allies. Wherever the Japanese discovered that this was not the case, they gave up in droves. Yet another consideration which caused some to seek death rather than surrender was the belief that death was the only means effectively to apologize to the emperor for military failure. Sometimes this requirement was thought to require the death of everyone and sometimes only a "token" death, usually the commander and his immediate staff.

Second, is prisoner immunity, in general, "absolute?" Can the killing of prisoners ever be morally justified? There are situations which would seem to permit the killing of prisoners. Suppose, for example, that one is fighting in a jungle war where there are no fixed lines and therefore no means of sending prisoners to the rear areas. Let us further suppose that if those captured are released they will quickly reassume combatant status. Here it seems there would be argument for killing them or for simply taking no prisoners if one then had to execute them. As with all matters in war, this is easier to say than to do, but it does seem to be possible to justify such action based upon the likelihood of prisoners returning to combatant status plus the question of what the enemy is likely to do with our people who fall into his hands. Such calculations are, of course, extremely difficult to make, particularly in the heat of battle, but it does appear that there could be conditions which would warrant overriding the principle of prisoner immunity. My guess is that, on the whole, these justifying situations have been and will be extremely rare in practice, but one ought not to deny that they could in principle exist. One way to deal with this problem, both prudentially and morally, might be to revive the nineteenth-century device of parole, whereby prisoners undertook in writing to return home and refrain from again becoming combatants. If this convention were to be adopted, it would then be possible to deal with prisoners even where there were no facilities to hold them.

The parole convention would not, however, permit us to come to grips with another difficult problem, that of what to do in a case where the combatant has been incapacitated and we are unable to take him prisoner, and yet we can kill him. The classic recorded instances of this possibility occurred during the Battle of Britain. This had to do with whether it was permissible to fire upon an enemy airman parachuting from a destroyed aircraft. If the airman was falling onto British soil, there was obviously no question he would be picked up and imprisoned; but what if he were falling into the sea where there was a possibility of being rescued by his own forces? Official policy on both sides opposed firing upon downed airmen, but individual pilots on both sides sometimes did so. Most R.A.F. pilots reasoned that it would simply not be right to kill an unarmed enemy who may or may not be rescued but who, in any case, was most probably wounded with the prospect of hours battling the elements. It just did not seem right to attack a man under those circumstances; and, of course, one never knew when the same fate might befall oneself. This seems to me to be about right. While one could not say that there will be absolutely no circumstances in which it would be right to fire on a downed airman, in general one ought to observe his immunity from attack, morally because the combatant has been removed from the man and prudentially because one would hope to be so treated oneself.

To illustrate the foregoing points I will consider two incidents in the fighting career of R.A.F. ace Robert Tuck. The first occurred at Dunkirk and involved Tuck's damaging a German fighter so badly that it was forced to land. Circling the downed enemy, Tuck saw the pilot climb from his burning craft and give a wave. Tuck banked his Spitfire and returned the gesture, whereupon the German whipped out a Mauser machine pistol and opened fire. Tuck immediately went into a dive, giving the German a full blast of all guns.

The second incident happened late one December day and is described as follows by Larry Forrester:

The man in the water was a German, the sole survivor of a Ju.88 which "Duke" Wolley, commander of 124 Squadron, and Tuck had shot down between them. He was over forty miles from the nearest land and there were no ships in sight. He had no dinghy. He had no hope.

He was dying slowly, miserably. He might last another ten, fifteen or twenty minutes—choking, threshing, growing numb and weak, so alone and so ridiculous in his helplessness. Every second would be an eternity of despair and torment. Tuck circled low, watching him, and thought: If that were me, down there, I know what I'd be praying for.

He called up his pilots—"Return to base. I'll stand by here . . . just in case." Just in case what? Could the sea change suddenly to summer warmth, or might a submarine pop up, or a flying boat swoop in to make the most miraculous landing of all time on those giant breakers . . . ? He knew he was fooling no one.

He was left alone with the German and he thought: If that were me down there . . . or if that man were my friend, an old and dear friend, instead of an anonymous enemy, God knows this is what I would want to happen. Yes, I am sure, I am sure. And so I will do it.

He widened his circle, turned in toward the man, heading downwind. He throttled back and put the nose down until the gunsight framed the tiny, bobbing target. He checked the turn and bank. His thumb moved on the little red button. Thank God, from here he couldn't see the man's face, only the top of the head, the bulky collar of the life jacket and the feebly flailing arm. He pressed the button.

The plumes of spray stood up, very straight and tall for a long time before the wind tore them, gradually pulled them aside to reveal—nothing but a wide white stain which the waves quickly broke up.

He thought: It was the right thing, the only thing to do. But I will tell no one, for some may not understand.

At the time it did seem right, it did seem the only thing. But later doubt came gnawing at his conscience, a voice that whispered sometimes in the night, whispered a shameful, ugly word. He has asked me to be completely honest about this incident, so I can tell you that today he still hears this voice occasionally, still has to reason with himself to dispel a feeling of guilt.

"I've never told anyone about this before—though I'm pretty sure my pilots had a shrewd idea what had happened after I sent them on ahead. It hasn't been easy to live with."[5]

In attempting to interpret and explain to the reader Tuck's reaction, Forrester makes the following comments:

How revealing that this one incident should haunt him! Here is a man who in the course of his career shot over thirty aircraft out of the sky, several of them as blazing deathtraps for crews of three or four enemy airmen—one of the many pilots whose guns attacked railway trains, waterfronts, factories and various other targets in occupied Europe, undoubtedly killing and wounding an unknown number of civilians—men, women, and let's face it, probably children. And all these years later, what is the one memory that hurts and worries him? The memory of that single German Flier, helpless in the water, whom he shot out of sheer mercy.

Why then need Tuck have had misgivings? The answer is that, like many other British fighter pilots, for all his flying days he clung to an antiquated code, and in many senses confused war with sport! As long as the contest was impersonal he was tiger-ishly aggressive and completely ruthless, but the moment his quarry changed from machine to man, the final whistle blew in his mind. There was, of course, the time at Dunkirk when he'd killed a Luftwaffe pilot on the ground, but then the damned fool had answered a friendly wave with defiant bullets—it was the German who'd broken the code. . . .[6]

Given the arguments which I have developed thus far, it is clear that it is Forrester and not Tuck who is confused. Indeed, in his attempted explanation Forrester unintentionally but gratuitously insults a group of exhausted and war-weary men who often had to make agonizing decisions with little time for reflection under brutal combat conditions. Forrester's argument here is that Tuck and others like him simply suffered from lack of imagination. Because

Tuck could *see* the downed German flier directly in front of him, the target suddenly became human and gave rise to doubts about the morality of killing, whereas if the target was a warehouse or an enemy aircraft, one could fire at *it* and repress the fact of its human occupancy. As for the flier at Dunkirk—well, he "broke the code."

Let us reconsider, in the light of just-war arguments, the three sorts of examples in Forrester's book. First, in the instance of the flier forced down at Durnkirk, Tuck assumed that the combatant was out of the man, and his wave symbolized that fact—a simple gesture but, under the circumstances, one of overwhelming importance in confirming the distinction between the bond of humanity which unites us all and the sometimes cruel necessity which leads men to become combatants. It was only when Tuck discovered that the combatant was *not* out of the man that he again targeted the combatant. This is a perfectly straightforward case of killing in war and, as we have seen, is different, given the intention and thrust of the action, from murder.

Next, Forrester lumps together the shooting down of enemy planes and the killing of civilians in raids. In the first instance we again have a perfectly straightforward example of targeting combatants. If they remove themselves from that role (by parachute) they are presumed immune from further attack. Dowding, in fact, issued a directive prohibiting the shooting of Germans bailing out over British Territory on the grounds that they would become prisoners, but said that the Germans should not be blamed for shooting *British* pilots bailing out over *British* territory on the grounds that they were certain to return to combat. It was reported that this evenhanded logic did not impress Dowding's fliers.[7]

To return to Tuck, it is inconceivable, as Forrester implies, that Tuck (and others) were somehow unaware that there were people in those planes, as they were themselves fliers, and who would be more acutely aware of those fellow mortals than their counterparts? As for the second instance, the target *was* a railway or a warehouse and, as we shall see in subsequent discussion, such incidental or collateral damage *may* be justified if the target is a vital one necessary to the prosecution of a justified war.

Finally, it was the incident of the German flier, totally incapacitated, dying in the water, which Tuck quite correctly perceived as constituting the moral problem. There was no way to describe what happened here in the idioms of the former examples: Tuck's bullets were directed at the man as a direct means of bringing his life to an end. Tuck hoped that his motives were good and that the killing could be justified, but he saw, perhaps only intuitively, the vast moral difference between directly willing the death of another and acting in such a way that death is an unintended consequence of trying to do something else; it is the difference between murder and killing in war.

Forrester's position is typical of those who fail to understand the centrality of intention with respect to moral judgments involving killing. He sees nothing but acts of violence resulting in dead bodies and assumes that they must, morally, all be the same.

What I have tried to show thus far is that understanding human action requires taking intention into account and that in the case of killing enemy soldiers the direction of the action is toward restraint of the combatant and not toward killing the man. This brings us to the second point I need to make about intention.

Aquinas draws a distinction between intended and unintended consequences of actions and calls the latter "accidents." This bit of scholastic terminology is apt to give the wrong impression about what is being claimed. Elizabeth Anscombe relates the story of the schoolboy who was greatly puzzled by his priest's statement that the people killed at Hiroshima all died by accident.[8] The boy, of course, understood the term in its common meaning as an expression of chance or fortune, as when we speak of a traffic accident. The traditional position on justified killing is obviously not claiming that what is beside the agent's intention is not a result of human action, sometimes foreseen, but only that the direction of the action is toward some other end. When the dentist goes into my mouth, his intention is to extract my tooth. The intense pain which I feel is foreseen by him and foreknown by him to be a result of his action, but it is not intended, in the sense that *if* he could drill the tooth without the incidental consequence of my pain, he would do so. This is the difference between dentistry as it is normally practiced and the use of dental procedures to torture people, that is, to inflict pain as such or to inflict it as a *means* to some other end. To the patient the distinction may seem entirely academic; in both cases there is a man in a white coat drilling teeth and thus causing pain. To an observer the two situations may appear identical, as in the earlier example of Smith and Jones. These are, however, obviously different actions, and what makes them different is not that in one case the pain is accidental (chance) and in the other it is not. Rather, in both cases the pain is a foreknown matter. In the dentist's case the pain is foreknown but unintended, and in the torturer's case it is foreknown and intended. The moral difference between tooth drilling and torture by tooth drilling is, thus, made intelligible by the principle of double effect: the torturer directly employs pain (or the threat of it) as a means to some other end; the dentist *accepts* the fact that pain will be a result of his action, not as a means to something else, but as a collateral consequence of the attempt to help the patient. This is not to say that torture might not under some extraordinary circumstances be justified but precisely that *it would have to be justified in a way that dentistry would never have to be.*

To generalize: The foregoing example is in support of the point that an action may have an unintended but foreknown consequence for which the agent will not be culpable. It will indeed be a result of his action but will not be intended as an end in itself or as a means to some other end. Applying this to the combat situation, we can say that the intention to restrain or incapacitate the combatant from doing what he is doing is compatible with the fore-knowledge that he will be killed.

The intention to incapacitate will entail that soldiers will provide the enemy with reasonable opportunity to remove themselves from the role of combatant and, if wounded, with facilities for humane treatment. But there is no culpability where for reasons of military necessity such conditions might not obtain. In the confusion of an advance it may not be possible to attend to prisoner immunity, or if the enemy refuses to surrender, then his death is a matter which he brings upon himself (this will be further explained below). A soldier fighting in a justified war must enter combat carrying with him the intention to incapacitate and not to kill, an intention which is compatible with the fore-knowledge that some will be killed. The *degree* to which this intention will be implemented is obviously contingent upon a great many variables, including such things as the type of warfare, terrain, weaponry, and even cultural attitudes toward the value of life. It must, however, be the case that no matter how many of these variables come into play, it will still be plausible for the individual combatant to claim that he is acting with the intention to incapacitate. Finally, it should not be supposed that the intention to incapacitate entails any naïve restrictions with respect to tactical matters; for example, the individual soldier cannot be required to avoid firing at vital areas of the human body or otherwise put himself at unreasonable risk.* At the same time, states do have an obligation to seek agreement on weapons which tend to create unnecessary damage, as in

---

*That is, a soldier may very well have to kill the aggressor in the course of attempting to incapacitate him, but that is something which the aggressor will bring upon himself. Soldiers will not, then, be understood as killing *in order* to incapacitate but as using their weapons with the intention of incapacitation, while knowing that in some circumstances the only weapon available will cause death, as when a soldier fires a machine gun at point-blank range. "Incapacitation" is, in my terminology, a state short of death. The soldier ought to intend the former but be prepared to *accept* the latter if he is given no choice.

the case of the convention banning the dumdum bullet, poison bullets, and bullets containing glass. There are a great number of weapons currently in use which are highly questionable in this respect, and one might expect future conventions to deal with them. Interestingly, considerable research is being undertaken to develop a workable incapacitating gas. This would certainly be the ideal solution to the problem of killing in war, and it is a line of research which is obviously entailed by *bellum justum.*

So far we have been discussing double effect exclusively in connection with the killing of enemy combatants in an attempt to deal with the criticism that all killing in war is murder. We must now tackle the "other half" of that criticism, namely, that the killing of noncombatants in war is murder. This is obviously a more difficult problem to come to grips with than the question of combatant deaths. For in the latter case the enemy soldier is armed and is personally directing acts of force against others. Although, as we have argued, in directing an act of force against an enemy combatant there should be no intention to kill the person, yet in the case of the aggressor there is an important sense in which he may be said to bring his own death upon himself, particularly in those cases where surrender is possible. A soldier fighting in a just cause may be forced to use weapons which will result in the death of the aggressor, but the aggressor will have participated directly in this outcome. A combatant may change his status by reverting to a noncombatant role; but if he refuses to do so, then much of the responsibility for what happens rests with him.

The problem of noncombatant immunity is frequently thought to center upon the difficulty of distinguishing a separate class of noncombatants, particularly in modern warfare. This is, I think, a large mistake, and it arises in part from an excessively literal reading of war solidarity propaganda. In fact, it is relatively easy to distinguish, in any historical war, whole classes of people who cannot, save in the inflamed world of the propagandist, be said to be combatants in any sense which would make them the object of attack. There will, as with every interesting distinction, be borderline cases. The criterion will be something like this: Generally speaking, classes of people engaged in occupations which they would perform whether or not a war were taking place, or services rendered to combatants both in war and out, are considered immune. This would exempt, for example, farmers and teachers (since education and food are necessities in and out of war) but not merchant sailors transporting war materiel or railway drivers in charge of munitions trains. In other words, the soldiers who are now eating and studying would have to do these things even if they were not soldiers, so that classes of people supplying those sorts of goods and services may be said to be immune from attack, whereas those who are engaged in the production and supply of goods used only in war are not immune. And, of course, certain classes of people may be said to be permanently noncombatant — young children, the mentally defective, and those who are in various ways physically incapacitated. Again, some "hard" or limiting cases will arise, particularly in guerrilla war, but they are less numerous than is sometimes supposed.

The *real* difficulty is not in delineating classes of individuals who merit immunity but in deciding what constitutes a direct attack upon them, for it is plausible to suppose that the deaths of noncombatants can be excused only if their deaths can be construed as collateral or beside the intention of the perpetrators. I want to tackle this problem by way of considering two examples, both of which involve a weapons system which is sometimes said to be indiscriminate. First, an example from World War II shows how, ideally, the principle of double effect ought to work in practice.

In 1944 the R.A.F. was carefully considering a plan to attack Gestapo headquarters in Copenhagen in order to destroy records of resistance activity in Denmark as well as to release captured resistance workers if possible. The officer in charge of the raid, Air Marshal Sir Basil Embry, was fully aware of the possibility that there might be non-combatant casualties: "As usual we had the target and the approaches to it modeled, and planned the operation with greatest care because the slightest error in navigation would cause heavy casualties among the Danes."[9]

There was also considerable anxiety over the fate of resistance workers held prisoner in the cells of Gestapo headquarters. It was difficult to imagine that many of them would survive a raid. A Danish officer attached temporarily to the operation put it in this way:

"Who knows—some might not be killed as happened at Aarhus, and anyhow their death will save many more Danish lives so don't worry."

I asked him about a house near the target which I thought almost certain to be damaged, and he replied with a grin, "The Germans use it for immoral purposes and so if one bomb hits it by accident, it would be excellent!"

All went well for the attack until one of the planes struck a bridge upright and crashed into a convent school. The second wave of aircraft, thinking this was the target, bombed the wreckage, causing loss of life to many innocent children. Naturally this unfortunate incident caused great sorrow and distress in the Group, but the Danes accepted it with brave and stoic hearts, and acclaimed the attack as a blow for freedom.[10]

In the event, the mission was a complete success. Shell House was totally demolished, and all Gestapo records were destroyed. All the resistance workers escaped, and twenty-six Gestapo personnel were killed.

The successive stages of this operation make it a good example of the principle of double effect in practice. There is first of all the intention that the action produce morally good consequences. The raid is carried out within the context of a justified war and is directed toward saving the lives of resistance workers and indirectly toward shortening the war. This is to be accomplished by directly attacking combatants and by taking reasonable precautions to avoid noncombatant casualties, even though these are expected. There are two further interesting attempts at discrimination. Concern over the possible death of resistance workers trapped in Gestapo cells arises but is dismissed on the implied grounds that these people are combatants, that they have placed themselves in a risk situation such that their deaths would be in the line of duty. The case of the house of ill repute is, however, an occasion for some uneasy jocularity. A direct attack is ruled out, but some residual question as to the noncombatant status of the inmates constrains the Danish officer to hope for an "accident." The death of the children is recognized for the evil which it is, but it is clearly understood by all to be collateral evil, beside the moral intention of the attackers.

By contrast, consider the practice at the other end of the scale of aerial warfare: saturation or terror bombing. As a case study in the banality of evil, it will be worthwhile to briefly consider the genesis of this practice in the 1930s.

With the formation of the Royal Air Force in 1918 as a separate service, an appropriate statement of its mission was devised as a means of ensuring its continuation as an independent body. It had previously been considered to be no more than a kind of aerial artillery, thus making air power subordinate to the needs and strategy of the army. The concept of strategic bombing was formulated as a means of convincing critics that the role of the air force was different in kind from those of the army and the navy. This theory is summed up by Noble Frankland:

The strategic air offensive is a means of direct attack on the enemy state with the object of depriving it of the means or will to continue the war. It may, in itself, be the instrument of victory or it may be the means by which victory can be won by other forces. It differs from all previous kind of armed attack in that it alone can be brought to bear immediately, directly and destructively against the heartland of the enemy. Its sphere of activity is, therefore, not only above, but also beyond that of armies or navies.[11]

So far so good. The operational implication of this was thought to be daylight attacks upon specific economic and military targets. The RAF had, in fact, virtually no experience in this type of warfare, but continuous harping on the theory allowed them to retain their independence against very heavy pressure during the interwar years.

By the outbreak of World War II it soon became evident that the proposed discriminate attacks upon military and economic targets by day were impossible due to the technical inability to place bombs accurately on small targets. As Liddell-Hart puts it:

Meanwhile the German bombing of Rotterdam on May 14, and of other cities subsequently, had begun to change the climate of opinion in Britain, and diminish repugnance to the idea of indiscriminate bombing. That change of feeling was much accentuated by the bombs that were dropped by error on London on August 24. All these cases were, actually, products of misinterpretation — if quite natural ones — as the Luftwaffe was still operating under orders to conform to the old, and longstanding, rules of bombardment, and exceptions hitherto arose from navigational mistakes. But they created a growing desire to hit back at German cities, and indiscriminately. Awareness that Bomber Command now constituted Britain's only offensive weapon in the near future, deepened both the instinct and the desire. Both were particularly evident in Mr. Churchill's attitude.

The change of view and attitude in the mind of the Air Staff, however, largely came from operational factors. Their weakening both to operational reality and to Churchill's pressure was shown in their directive of October 30, 1940, ordering that oil targets be attacked on clear nights and cities on other nights. That embodied, quite clearly, their acceptance of the idea of indiscriminate, or "area bombing."[12]

The inaccuracy of British bombing, plus the impossibility of conducting daylight raids because of German fighters, gradually pushed the Air Staff in the direction of night raids which targeted whole cities:

As the inaccuracy of British bombing became clearer, increasing emphasis was given by the Air Staff to the effect on the morale of the civil population — in a word, to terrorization. Breaking the enemy people's will to fight was becoming as important as breaking the enemy force's means to fight.[13]

At the same time that this new strategy of area bombing was being put into operation, Coastal Command was suffering from an acute shortage of aircraft in its battle to keep the sea lanes to Britain open. The German submarine campaign came within an ace of success and would have lost the war for Britain. And yet Bomber Command fought fanatically to prevent aircraft being transferred to Coastal Command on the grounds that their retention would allow them to be used "offensively" against the enemy's heartland, whereas Coastal Command could only use them "defensively"!

Despite growing doubts about the efficacy of strategic bombing, both physical and moral, it gradually became the officially sanctioned position:

As a new directive to Bomber Command on February 14, 1942, emphasized that the bombing campaign was now to be "focused on the morale of the enemy civil population and in particular, of the industrial workers." That was to be the "primary object." Thus terrorization became without reservation the definite policy of the British government, although still disguised in answers to Parliamentary questions.[14]

A series of massive and costly raids were mounted in pursuit of this policy, culminating in the Battle of Berlin, which ran from November 1943 to March 1944. It was undertaken largely to please Stalin, who wanted to have Berlin bombed. Sixteen raids were made on the capital as well as other attacks on Stuttgart, Frankfurt, and Leipzig for a total of twenty thousand sorties: "The results of this massive offensive turned out different from those predicted by 'Bomber' Harris. Germany was not brought to her knees, nor Berlin, whereas British losses became so heavy that the campaign had to be abandoned."[15]

Despite the enormously increased capacity for precision bombing which developed as the war progressed, Bomber Command continued to adhere to its policy of saturation attacks long after it had become clear that the Germans were not going to be defeated by terror any more than were the British. It also became clear that the physical damage to Germany was not justified by the cost in lives and planes:

In 1943, a total of 2,000,000 tons of bombs was dropped on Germany—nearly five times as much as in 1942. Yet German productivity rose to new heights, thanks largely to the reorganization carried out by Albert Speer, while air raid precaution measures and the German ability of quick recovery prevented any crisis in either morale or production. The increased output of guns, aircraft, tanks and submarines contributed to the overall 50 percent rise of armaments production in 1943.[16]

The ability to hit precise targets, plus the clear need to hit oil and communications targets, makes the decision to carry on as usual even more puzzling:

In view of this new capacity for precision bombing with little opposition, it is questionable whether it was wise, either operationally or morally, for Bomber Command to devote 53 per cent of its bombs in this period to town areas, compared to only fourteen per cent to oil plants and fifteen per cent to transportation targets.

The ratio in the Americans' targeting was essentially different. Their idea of aiming to hit Germany's known weak points was more sensible than that of trying to ensure that every bomb hit something, and somehow weaken Germany. It also avoided the increasing moral censure that Harris's policy was to attract.[17]

After much debate a policy of selective targeting was agreed upon but not carried out because of Harris's refusal to do so, backed by his threat to resign. In the end it was decided to attempt both strategic and precision bombing:

The most controversial aspect is the deliberate revival of terrorization. It was revived largely to please the Russians. On January 27, 1945, Harris was given instructions to carry out such blows—which thus became second in priority to oil targets, and ahead of communications and other objectives. As a consequence, the distant city of Dresden was subjected to a devastating attack in mid-February—with the deliberate intention of wreaking havoc among the civil population and refugees—striking at the city centre, not the factories or railways.[18]

The first point about this example is that the policy of terrorization was not in the initial stages a result of malice, but, rather, it arose from a simple possession of a means which for technical reasons could be used in no other way. Of course, a *decision* had to be made to actually use it, but that decision was helped along by the vast amount of money, time, energy, and argument which had been invested in the bombers. This should sound a clear warning against the dangers of even possessing weapons which have the potential for indiscriminate use. It becomes all too easy to find good reasons for using them.

But the most important fact is that, moral questions aside, terrorization was unsuccessful as a tactic. I believe we can safely generalize from this example and say that such will always be the case; not "always" in the sense that it is absolutely impossible to *imagine* a case, but in the light of historical experience we can judge that such tactics ought to be avoided because they are counterproductive. While *bellum justum* insists that direct attacks upon noncombatants are morally wrong, it also carries with it the understanding that what is morally wrong is likely to be imprudent. This conjunction is clearly demonstrated by strategic bombing.

First, terrorization did not work. It has been proven time and again that direct attacks upon noncombatants simply harden the will of the enemy to resist and thereby create a climate in which war tends to become "total." As *bellum justum* has always firmly insisted, there are no shortcuts in war. Attempts to win a trial of strength by attacking a whole people results in the prolongation of the war.

Second, the precedents set by terrorization have made possible the transition to massive nuclear retaliation. Officially sanctioned policies of direct attacks by air upon noncombatants has done incalculable damage, for once a decision is taken to short-cut the rules of war, it is very difficult to go back. This is one of the cruelist ironies of modern history. The decision in World War II to shorten the war by directly attacking noncombatants as a means of terrorizing them into submission leads inexorably to the question: If we are allowed to attack some noncombatants, why not *all* of them? Nuclear weapons provide the means. By abandoning restraint in what appeared to be a good cause, we now risk total destruction.

Between the Copenhagen raid and the Dresden raid there will be many difficult or borderline cases. There is obviously no way of specifying the precise point beyond which it becomes implausible to claim that civilian damage is beside the intention of the attacker, but it would be absurd to suppose that we ought for *that* reason to abandon the distinction. At the risk of laboring the point: The concepts "night" and "day" are meaningful and useful even though "dawn" and "twilight" may be ultimately defined arbitrarily.

Now the rule forbidding the deliberate killing of noncombatants also has a purely moral defense. This argument is stated succinctly by Michael Walzer:

The rule (noncombatant immunity) can also be defended because of the intrinsic value it attaches to human personality. It requires that we pay attention to what men and women are actually doing, that we regard and treat them as responsible agents. So we fight soldiers, who are armed and trained and committed to fight us (whether or not they are actually engaged in combat). But we do not fight civilians who, whatever their hopes for our destruction, are not engaged in bringing it about. Obviously this defense is challenged by the claim, frequently made, that there are no noncombatants in modern war. This claim is certainly exaggerated (small children are always, one might say eternally, noncombatants) but I am inclined to think it is false unless stated very modestly indeed. In modern war there are fewer noncombatants than ever before. This minimal claim follows from the conventional recognition that munitions workers are at least partial combatants, subject to attack in their factories (though not at home)—for modern war requires a very large industrial plant. But there remain vast numbers of people who are not engaged in any activity properly called warmaking. In the words of G. E. M. Anscombe, they "are not fighting and not engaged in supplying those who are with the means of fighting." Intentional attacks upon them do not seem to me properly called combat.

Such attacks victimize and exploit innocent people, turning them into means to an end which, it must be stressed again, they were not opposing in any military way, though they may have opposed it in other ways when they were alive. In the bombing of cities, civilians are effectively claimed as hostages by the enemy and, like more conventional hostages, are degraded from moral agents to human pawns even before they are murdered.[19]

Two conclusions can be reached from all of this. To begin with, in a justified war combatants are the objects of attack by other combatants. In this context the use of force is directed toward incapacitation and not toward killing. Combatant deaths may be foreseen, but this is compatible with the intention to incapacitate. Second, noncombatant immunity is presupposed and will be stated in absolute terms. Noncombatant deaths may be foreseen but may also be regarded as collateral damage if they occur in the context of a justified war as outlined above. The critic's error in both cases is to run together intention and foreknowledge or expectation.

Throughout the foregoing discussion, I have refrained from making any reference to "the innocent," despite the fact that most of the current debate on the morality of war has been about treatment of innocent parties. This seems to me to represent a major confusion which has quite unnecessarily complicated the issue. I want now to show why this is so; but as a preliminary, I will have to discuss briefly the concept of innocence.

There are essentially two senses in which a person may be said to be innocent. First there is the legalistic sense, where our interest lies in discovering who did x and whether or not the act was intentional. That is, here we are typically concerned with the kind of questions which arise in legal proceedings. Thus the claim of innocence in this context means either that the accused did not perform the action or that he did it but ought to be judged not culpable by virtue of some set of excusing conditions provided in law. This notion of innocence carries with it the two prior assumptions: that the parties in litigation are equal with respect to their capacity for responsibility and that the forthcoming verdict will be rendered on the merits of the case and not upon some view respecting the nature of the persons involved. It may turn out that they are in fact not so equal, as in the case of insanity or minority, but we begin on the assumption that they are. For it makes sense to say that two persons have competing rights only if they are both in some fundamental way equal with respect to capacity for responsibility.

The second sense in which people are sometimes said to be innocent has to do not with the question of responsibility (who did x and what were his intentions?) but with the issue of the relative capacities for responsibility of the parties concerned. This I shall call natural innocence as it has to do with capacities as opposed to actions.

Michael Walzer has tried to get at the essence of the concept of natural innocence by remarking, "Children are *eternally* innocent." What this means can be understood as follows: In the evolution of unborn children to adult status there are levels or stages representing increased capacity for responsibility. Obviously these stages are not clearly defined, and in some cases they may have to be arbitrarily decided with respect to boundaries. In each stage actual responsibilities may be said to increase with a judged capacities, but these are compensated by increased rights and privileges. It is understood in these terms that as the stages represent a progression in intellectual and moral development (with corresponding advantages) those in more advanced stages are, in fact, responsible for those in lower stages. *Within* a given stage the concept of legal innocence may be applied either formally or informally. That is, within each stage persons may be judged as having the same capacity for responsibility and, therefore, may be said to have competing rights, but there is no sense in which rights compete across boundaries where persons do not share some minimal capacity for responsibility.

The concept of natural or "eternal" innocence suggests a general responsibility toward those who are not responsible, in the sense of lacking capacity for responsibility or as having diminished responsibility. The distinction here is between being innocent of causing a particular injury (the agent did not perform x, or he did perform it but is excused) and an innocence which presupposes disparate levels of responsibility with the implied duty of seeing to the interests of those who cannot see to their own.

Having delineated these two senses of innocence, one pertaining to actions and the other to capacities, I contend that neither of these aspects has a great deal to do with the problem of just conduct in war. It is *combatants* who are the objects of attack in war, and, therefore, moral distinctions will center upon that notion rather than innocence. This is necessarily the case, since war is a contest of strength, an arbitrament of arms carried out under the direction of moral and political aims. Both defenders and attackers of *bellum justum* have tended hopelessly to confuse the issue by making innocence, and not combatancy, central. As an example of this confusion, I quote, at length, a passage from Joseph Margolis's book *Negativities.* In the chapter entitled "War" he says this:

One of the favorite issues that the genteel discussion of war has insisted on concerns the treatment of innocent parties. Miss Anscombe, registering the prevailing view, says that it is murderous to attack innocent people. The difficulty with this pronouncement is that it is vacuously true. She also says that "innocence is a legal notion," but if it is, then apart from appeal to a higher law, the very idea of an innocent party will be controlled by the overriding notion of how to justify a given war. For example, in a racial or ethnic war or even in a more conventional war between states that is expected to run for generations, there is no clear sense in which, say, bearing children, the future warriors of an enemy power, can be irresistably discounted as the activities of noncombatants. What is true of women and children in this regard is true, *a fortiori,* of factory workers, Red Cross personnel, priests, and the like.

Constraints on attacking this or that fraction of an enemy population depend at least on the clarity with which a distinctly professionalized army may be specified: Talk about the people's militia, treat every infant as a budding soldier, organize the nation's farmers as fighting soldiers, and you will have blurred the very basis on which the older distinctions between combatants and noncombatants were drawn. That the United States had difficulty in enlisting public support for bombing the North Vietnamese countryside is a concession of culture lag, not to the persistence of an indisputably defensible doctrine. At any rate, in the face of novel forms of war and of the apparently sincere rejection of restraints, that in more conventional war were thought to bind the behavior of combatants, it is difficult to see that the old constraints can be merely assumed to be fair. What is the reason for thinking that newer views about what is admissible in newer wars ought to conform to what, in an earlier time, was taken for granted?[20]

It will be noticed that Margolis moves easily from a discussion of innocence to talking about noncombatants. No attempt is made to distinguish between innocence and noncombatancy (or between guilt and combatancy). He *appears* to use them interchangeably, presumably in the belief that they are the same. These concepts differ importantly in the following ways:

First, in terms of our distinction between natural and legal innocence, young children may be described as naturally innocent and will thus form a permanent subclass of noncombatants.

Second, a combatant may be legally innocent though still an appropriate target for attack. For a person might have opposed the war but had been conscripted upon to fight upon threat of death. In such a case he would, in the language of the Nuremburg Tribunal, "have no moral choice." Qua person, he may not be attacked, but in his role as combatant he may. Thus, combatant status is in some circumstances compatible with legal innocence.

Third, it is also the case that guilt is compatible with being a noncombatant. For a person might have taken a leading role in starting an unjustified war but no part at all in fighting it or in supporting it. He might not even be present in the area of combat. In other cases, a person may support the war but, while remaining in the combat area, continue to perform tasks which would have to be performed even in peacetime, such as teaching or farming.

Fourth, there are the obvious cases where a person may be both guilty *and* a combatant but, as I shall argue, nothing special seems to follow from this conjunction as far as concerns our treatment of him in combat. For he is guilty qua person and not qua combatant. It is the distinction between a person and the function or role he may be serving which makes any identification of innocence with noncombatancy and guilt with combatancy wrongheaded. This is so because, typically, guilt and innocence are descriptions appropriate to whole persons, whereas combatancy and noncombatancy are functions or roles which people fulfill in an institutional sense. Thus, it is appropriate to speak of penalizing a football player for an infraction of the rules in his role as player, but of his manager punishing *him* for his refusal to turn up at practice. This distinction between punishment and penalty is important, for it brings out differences which Margolis's treatment obscures (though, ironically, he employs this same distinction in his chapter on punishment). Typically, anyone transgressing a rule in his capacity as role player (motorist, football player, teacher, soldier) is penalized, or perhaps censured, but not punished. Guilt and innocence, on the other hand, are correctly ascribed to persons qua persons, because it is only under that description that they can be said to cause harm in a way that would deserve punishment. Their failure to conform to the prescriptions of a particular role or function does not presuppose that any particular harm has been done. The importance of this distinction is that it makes possible different moral assessments of a person's conduct qua person and qua combatant, with the result that the treatment we accord him will also be relevantly varied.

Finally, there are cases where a person may be both legally innocent and a noncombatant. Immunity from direct attack is guaranteed here much in the same way as for the child.

To bring to bear an earlier argument: Traditional just-war theory distinguishes persons qua persons and persons qua combatants, and it makes this distinction central to its justification of the use of force. Specifically, the death of no *person* should be willed. This maxim constitutes a moral precondition for soldiers fighting in a justified war. The task of assessing guilt or innocence is not the soldier's function. His target is the combatant in the person and not the person qua person. This is not to say that questions of guilt and innocence are of no significance but only that judgments of guilt and innocence (with appropriate punishment) have as their subject matter the whole person and not the person qua combatant. The intention of war is not punishment. War is a morally justified arbitrament of arms aimed at resolving by means of discriminate and proportional force an injustice which is incapable of resolution by other means. I am aware that many traditional theorists of *bellum justum* employ the idioms of culpability, but I believe my interpretation retains the essence of the doctrine while avoiding the problems with such language.

With respect to the whole problem of innocence and guilt, we may briefly summarize thus: To begin with, in targeting the combatant and not the person, we leave *open* the question of innocence. This means that our concern is to incapacitate the combatant, not to kill or punish the person. Recalling the distinction between doing x that y may result and doing x knowing that y will result, the killing of the enemy soldier may be accepted if that is the only means to remove him from the role of combatant. This is the distinction between killing in war and murder, and it also provides the moral basis for taking prisoners. For if a soldier surrenders (or is otherwise incapacitated), he removes himself from the role of combatant; and as it is not the province of soldiers to render judgment of guilt or innocence, he is returned to the status of person. If the distinction between persons and combatants were not pre-supposed, there would be no moral objection to killing all prisoners or to refusing to take prisoners.

Furthermore, the distinction between combatants and noncombatants is central. Margolis's suggestion that *every-one* might be regarded as a combatant is defective. Quite apart from his running together innocence and noncom-batancy, he (and others) take much too seriously the war-solidarity rhetoric of contemporary guerrilla warriors. Such people will necessarily seek to construe the activities of every man, woman, and child as combatancy, even though at wildly varying degrees. This ploy is obviously necessary in the absence of a regular army adequate to the task, but it must be emphasized that it *is* mainly rhetoric. Even in a war such as that in Vietnam there were millions of people who could in no meaningful sense of combatancy be said to be engaged in the war effort. For them the war was a wholly meaningless cataclysm equivalent to a natural disaster. This gap between reality and rhetoric is nowhere more clearly seen than in the reaction of some Western antiwar groups to the MyLai atrocity. From one point of view, these groups had nothing but praise for the solidarity of the whole Vietnamese people as a "single army" in their struggle against the invader; but in response to Lt. Calley's hideous deeds they, too, were horrified at the killing of "innocent women and children who had nothing to do with the war." One cannot have it both ways. In a curious sense Calley also interiorized the same rhetoric—and per-haps that is its chief danger. It may well give incompetent and evil men, masquerading as soldiers, the justification for killing people who are in reality noncombatants.

Finally, the natural innocence of young children as such gives them no special protection not available to other non-combatants; it only means that they are necessarily non-combatant. While children and other noncombatants may not be made the object of a direct attack, there may be cases in which the death of a noncombatant will have to be accepted as incidental to some other result. There is a fine line, but there *is* a line between the foreseen death of noncombatants during a bombing raid whose purpose is the destruction of a vital target and the foreseen death of noncombatants who are themselves the target of a bombing attack whose purpose is the spreading of terror.

In a later chapter I will have more to say about the prudential aspects of *bellum justum,* but I want to mention it here in reference to the Margolis quotation. Margolis's description of just-war arguments as "genteel" reflects the widespread view that such arguments are essentially otherworldly. On the contrary, the upholders of justice in war intend to reflect the prudential concerns of men and societies and to show that here at least there is no divergence between morality and interest. The prudent society will necessarily seek to use force in a discriminate and proportional way. The prudent society will concern itself with the interests of those who cannot see to their own interests and will generate the concepts of combatancy and noncombatancy, for the prudent society will realize that to do otherwise will invite the opponent to respond in kind, creating an escalation of arbitrary, indiscriminate, and unrestrained violence which cannot serve the purpose of morality or prudence.

If the principle of noncombatant immunity is now intelligible, we may turn to the question of its status. This has been an intensely discussed issue in contemporary ethical theory. The usual scenario is for defenders of the principle of noncombatant immunity to begin by declaring roundly that there is an "absolute prohibition against making a direct attack upon the innocent" or that "evil must never be done that good may come of it," and the like. The critic then points out that the consequences of such a priorism would be morally disastrous. He is then likely to produce a series of now familiar examples of the form, "Suppose a mad scientist threatened to destroy the entire universe unless we agree to torture a young child to death. Surely it would be grossly immoral to refuse to do so. Only someone equally as mad as the mad scientist would stick to principle in a case like this."

Defenders of noncombatant immunity have consistently swallowed the bait and have attempted to save the argument in one of two ways:

1. Sometimes they dismiss the critic by simply denying that such a situation could ever arise. This is the "fantastic example" rejoinder. Such cases, it is argued, are preposterous and are typical of philosophers' fantasies bearing no relation to the real world. Thus, we can ignore them.

2. Sometimes it is said that, even if such examples should come to pass, we would need to have more information about the situation. This is the "insufficient data" rejoinder. So, staying with the example, even if we were convinced that the mad scientist possessed such a device, we might try other means of saving the universe such as assassination or capture rather than giving in to him.

The trouble with the first of these attempts is that it tacitly admits that *if* such examples did exist, they would be relevant. The charge of "fantastic examples" gives the game away because it means that defender is taking into account consequences; he has implicitly recognized a challenge to his position but simply *refuses to believe* that such a situation could come about. Yet clearly the refusal to believe that there could be such a situation implies that if there were it would be relevant. As for the "insufficient data" reply, no matter how much additional data is supplied, the critic can always quite reasonably construct his example in such a way as to limit the alternatives in order to create the required dilemma.

It has been quite generally supposed, therefore, that some form of utilitarianism must be triumphant in this matter. I wish to contest this apparent victory and, in what follows, I shall consider two versions of utilitarianism as they have been applied to the problem of noncombatant immunity. First it is necessary to say something in general about utilitarianism. The idea that it is possible to stipulate the maximization of interests (pleasure, happiness, and so on) as *the* criterion of correct moral behavior arose, historically, as an answer to the problem of the supposed disappearance of generally agreed upon objective moral standards. But such a program is, in effect, meaningless. For the injunction to measure and compute what is good in a manner which would make it possible to "maximize" it would require that human beings had some single end toward which all their actions should be inexorably directed. Alternatively, human actions and goals, so obviously variegated, would have to be conceived as sharing some common factor which would allow the operation of a calculus. But even the most cursory experience of human goods should dispel any such fantasies. Human goods are such that it makes no sense to say that they are either subsumable under one heading or are commensurable in a way that would allow their maximization. This fact is nearly always recognized by utilitarians themselves (such as Mill) when they distinguish between "higher" and "lower" pleasures, desires, interests, and so forth.

If human life in all its many forms is a fundamental value, a good in itself, how is it possible to *measure* such a thing so that one might calculate that the lives of this group of innocent people are to sacrificed to save another (larger?) group of lives? My act of torturing the young child to death in order to bring about the "consequence" of saving the universe would be a correct description only if were possible to measure human goods in the required way. The act of torturing the child has the "consequence" of killing in a brutal manner an innocent child. The salvation of the universe (if it happens) would be the result of another discrete act (that of the madman) which would be only one of the innumerable possible outcomes of the act of killing.

Now we have already seen that consequences, even to the extent that they can be "foreseen as certain," cannot be *com-*

mensurably evaluated, which means that "net beneficial consequences" is a literally absurd general objective or criterion. It only remains to note that a man who thinks that his rational responsibility is to be always doing and pursuing good, and is satisfied by a commitment to act always for the best consequences, is a man who treats every aspect of human personality (and indeed, therefore, treats himself) as a utensil. He holds himself ready to do *anything* (and thus makes himself a tool for all those willing to threaten sufficiently bad consequences if he does not cooperate with them).[21]

I want now to consider two versions of the utilitarian argument as applied to war. The first is a straightforward example of what might be called "orthodox" utilitarianism.

If we deliberately bomb civilian targets, we do not pretend that civilians are combatants in any simple fashion, but argue that this bombing will terminate hostilities more quickly, and minimize all around suffering. It is hard to see how any brand of utilitarian will escape Miss Anscombe's objections. We are certainly killing the innocent . . . we are not killing them for the sake of killing them but to save the lives of other innocent people. Utilitarians, I think, grit their teeth and put up with this as the logic of total war. Miss Anscombe, and anyone who thinks like her, surely has to redescribe the situation to ascribe guilt to the civilians or else she has to refuse to accept this sort of military tactics as simply wrong.[22]

This argument seems wrongheaded. The focus of the utilitarian argument in favor of killing one innocent person in order to save the lives of many and to "terminate hostilities more quickly and minimize all around suffering" is absurdly narrow and abstract. In the first place, there is no logical way to determine which of the various "principles" of maximized good is the correct one. Certainly there is no way on purely utilitarian grounds for preferring any particular one of the following: overall utility, average utility, maxmin, or equal amounts. But until we know which principle of distribution of goods is the correct one, then the slogan "The greatest good for the greatest number" makes no sense.

Furthermore, the claim that utilitarians must simply "grit their teeth" and accept the "logic" of total war reveals, I suspect, the fact that what is crucial in decisions to slaughter innocent people is not the utilitarian calculus at all but a desire for a particular outcome — in this case, a shortcut to ending the war. Having decided upon this objective, it becomes easy to ignore questions of justice to individuals and to focus upon "good" and "bad" consequences for effecting or failing to effect the desired conclusion.

Thus the "calculus" is forced through to provide a determinate solution (the quickest, cheapest way of getting what was first focused upon: hence the forced collectivization and liquidation of the farmers, the nuclear or firestorm bombing of the enemy's hostage civilians, the inquisitorial torture of suspects or informers, the fraudulent cover-up and obstruction of legal process, the abortion of unborn, and "exposure" of newly-born children . . .). Of course, by focusing on some other alternatives, and on the life possibilities of the proposed victims, and so on, one can in every case find reasons to condemn the favored action "on consequentialist grounds." But in truth both sets of calculations, in such cases are equally senseless. What generates the "conclusions" is always something other than the calculus: an overpowering desire, a predetermined objective, the traditions or conventions of the group.[23]

For these reasons I should argue that *orthodox* utilitarian arguments applied to the problem of noncombatant immunity fail through incoherence and irrelevance.

I want now to turn to a recent and ingenious recasting of the utilitarian position. I refer to the argument of Michael Walzer in *Just and Unjust Wars.* He begins his book with a firm commitment to the existence of human rights. While these are by him undefined, Walzer regards them as a fundamental datum of the moral life. They may be overridden, but never bargained away, utilitarian-style. Rights are never simply disposable in pursuit of some scheme for "maximizing" good. However, Walzer does believe that there are, in principle, conditions which would justify the *overriding* of the rights of the noncombatants. These conditions are three:

1. Before we could justifiably murder civilians, we would have to be faced with a threat to our security describable only in the idioms of ultimate evil. The threat would have to be such that *our* defeat would not merely result in the substitution of one conventional power structure for another, but in the triumph of evil—the coming to power of a regime of such unutterable awfulness that the result could only be a negation of all moral and civic virtue (including noncombatant immunity). It will, no doubt, sometimes be the case that inflamed emotions, reinforced by propaganda, will lead nations to falsely characterize their enemies as absolutely evil. But this kind of error cannot change the fact that nothing short of a threat to the basis of the moral life itself would justify direct attacks upon civilians.

2. The threat of ultimate evil must be accompanied by the absence of any other means to effectively combat it. The threat alone is not a sufficient condition for overriding noncombatant immunity *if* the evil can be thwarted by conventional military means. This condition will apply even where the "amount of suffering" or "lives lost" or "time consumed" will be *greater* where conventional means are employed.

3. The threat and imminence of overwhelming evil would not, by itself, justify the murder of noncombatants unless there was a reasonable certainty that this tactic would be successful in thwarting the event.

Thus, we must hew to the principle of noncombatant immunity as if it were an absolute principle up to the point where the foregoing three conditions obtain, at which point we become utilitarians and make our calculations accordingly.

Walzer's position here is obviously extremely attractive, as it appears to combine the best features of both utilitarianism and absolutism. He refuses to stand on principle, whatever the consequences, by providing reasonably clear conditions for breaking the rule of noncombatant immunity. This satisfies the utilitarian requirement that no one can reasonably hold that any moral principle is unbreakable in all circumstances. At the same time there is a nod in the direction of the absolutist. His claims are recognized in the argument that rights are not up for bargaining in terms of some sliding scale. They can only be overridden, not bargained away. Indeed, Walzer might be termed a de facto absolutist, since it is extremely unlikely that there should be a historical conjunction of *all* three of those conditions which Walzer claims are necessary for violating the principle of noncombatant immunity.

As appealing as Walzer's solution is, I believe that it will not, in the end, do. First, it is not clear to me whether Walzer intends his argument about noncombatant immunity to be a theory (or a part of a theory) or simply a piece of casuistry applied to a quite specific situation. When he speaks of "wagering" against the rules of war under some circumstances, is he enunciating general criteria or simply saying that under certain extraordinary circumstances one might break the rules? To put the matter differently, is Walzer prepared to hold himself ready to do *anything* in a situation of "supreme emergency"? Are there any limits to what he would be prepared to do in order to combat "absolute" evil? It is very important that we have answers to these questions, since unless we know how far Walzer would be prepared to go, what exactly he would be prepared to do, we cannot possibly assess how serious he is about such terms as "absolute" and "supreme." If we cannot do that, there is no way to evaluate his argument.

I suspect that Walzer is an absolutist manqué. He sees clearly that rights are not up for bargaining, but he is prepared under circumstances of "supreme emergency" to damage these rights in order to maximize good. Rights are so important that they can be damaged only under threat of "absolute evil," but all this seems largely a matter of definition. Of course, one is inclined to say that absolute rights could be overridden only under conditions of absolute evil. But what is this? The only example Walzer gives is Hitler, and even then he expresses reservations. If human good could be maximized (which it cannot), it would still have to be argued that the saturation bombing of German civilians would be the most efficient way to accomplish the destruction of "absolute" evil. As I have shown in an earlier discussion of the saturation bombing of Germany, that tactic was neither efficient nor, in the end, successful. Thus Walzer's thesis seems vague and lacking in historical instances. I believe that Walzer is torn between his correct perception that life is a basic human value not to be directly attacked and a peculiarly liberal tendency to associate the concept of "maximization" with that of "sharing." It is perhaps understandable that one should make what might seem a logical move from the idea that x is a basic human value to the conclusion that x should be "maximized." It is then easy to accept the corollary that this may have to be done by "sacrificing" some of x, but as I have argued above, such a procedure is incoherent.

Walzer argues that the time may come when we will have to wager a "determinate crime" (the murder of innocent people) against an "immeasurable" evil (say, the triumph of Hitler). But on my argument this gets thing precisely backward. It is impossible to measure the worth of a human life. How does one go about "determining" for purposes of calculation what a single life, the source and precondition of genuine human flourishing, is worth? The triumph of Hitler, on the other hand, *is* roughly calculable, otherwise people like Walzer would not be tempted to do such terrible things to stop him. Thus there is at least *one* absolute human right—the right not to be directly killed as a means to something else, and, thus, the principle of noncombatant immunity must be regarded as absolute. I shall continue this theme in the following discussion of nuclear war.

Chapter 3

Nuclear Weapons and Insurgency

WHEN critics argue that *bellum justum* is irrelevant to the conditions of modern war, they usually mean those two forms of conflict which have come to the fore in this century: nuclear and guerrilla warfare. On the surface these two seem poles apart — the gleaming missile in the antiseptic silo, deep underground, poised to strike at the enemy's heartland, contrasted with the peasant, armed with a rifle, slogging his way through a steaming jungle. What we seem to see is the revival of an almost primitive mode of warfare set alongside the ultimate in technological refinement. But what they have in common, what ties them together from the perspective of *bellum justum*, is that they both tend to enlarge the target to include, specifically, noncombatants; and they both tend to move warfare away from a contest of strength and in the direction of a contest of wills.

Let us first consider the question of nuclear war. The underlying theory of nuclear deterrence is that nations will find it politically impossible to go to war while the threat of annihilation hangs over their heads. Thus, peace is to be brought about through a balance of terror in which both sides make clear their willingness to retaliate massively with nuclear weapons. This point of view was generated in the 1950s, essentially by American and British strategists of a liberal persuasion in pursuit of what they perceived to be the morally desirable and practically possible goal of perpetual peace. This line of thinking may be traced back to the eighteenth-century Enlightenment philosophers (Kant, in particular), for whom war was in principle not a feature of statecraft. That is, war was not one among many

71

considered means of effecting state interest but was, on the contrary, the ultimate expression of irrationality and aberrant behavior. The solution to the problem of war was thus seen to turn on the possibility of making reason felt in the conduct of statecraft. This was to be accomplished either by tinkering with the internal structures of states (in Kant's case, by making them all republics) or by overcoming the "anarchy" of international society by bringing all the states under one civil society.

By the 1950s it was clear to many strategists that these two avenues to peace were closed. This did not mean, however, that the goal of perpetual peace was to be abandoned; rather, it was to be brought into being precisely by utilizing that very irrationality which had for so long been seen as the main stumbling block to peace. In an ironic twist, the new guiding conception became "the rationality of irrationality." What this means is, roughly, that because men will not become rational, in the sense that they will act morally in light of what any rational being could consistently will for all, we will *make* the nations behave rationally by publicly declaring our willingness to be irrational, escalating to the level of ultimate irrationality if necessary. If other nations know that we are prepared to be irrational, to destroy the entire world, and if they know that we have so arranged things that we have no option but to be irrational (that is, no one may count on our being rational), then peace will be assured. It will be assured because any potential enemy will realize that total destruction is a matter which will come automatically, for we will have no other options open to us. And all of *this* was claimed to be rational, because peace could be certainly obtained in no other way.

The opposition to this view was led by Raymond Aron, who argued that nuclear weapons have not deterred war but only nuclear war, thus far. Nuclear weapons have themselves in no fundamental way altered the practice of diplomacy and international politics. As the use of such weapons systems would be suicidal, nations have simply not used them; but by the same token, the balance of terror has not produced perpetual peace. War is a necessary aspect of international relations which will find some means of expression even in a world armed with hydrogen bombs. In Aron's words: "Relations between sovereign states may be more or less bellicose; they are never *essentially* or *ultimately* peaceful. To eliminate the possibility of war is to deprive states of the right to be the ultimate judges of what defense of their interests or their honor demands."[1]

Aron's claim is also a premise which *bellum justum* will grant. To attempt to eliminate the *possibility* of war while leaving the nation-state system in being is a dangerous illusion, particularly when the means for doing so threaten the destruction of the world. If war is justified, then it must be the expression of a rational policy; but no policy could be served by massive retaliation. There are here no "issues" in any rational sense which could be settled by such war, and insofar as war is defined as a trial of strength between combatants, nuclear war is not worthy of the name. In the attempt to constrain violence we have stressed the importance of nations tacitly agreeing on what will count as having been defeated. If force is justified, there must be some prior conception of what will count as the resolution of the conflict. Now, we have seen that the traditional conception of war as a trial of strength attempts, at one and the same time, to constrain the spread of violence by limiting fighting to a class of combatants and, thereby, to specify the conditions which will determine the outcome — the defeat of one of the armies. To put the point differently, war has traditionally been seen as an *agreement* between two nations to submit an outstanding issue to the arbitrament of arms, an arbitrament to be safeguarded from escalation by confining it to combatants clearly specified. Peace returns when it becomes evident that one side has miscalculated the relative power situation. *If* force can be justified, then this approach is essentially rational, both in its attempt to constrain violence and in its refusal to embark upon war save in pursuit of some goal which might reasonably be expected to ensue from a trial of strength.

The problem with massive nuclear retaliation is that it inevitably pushes us away from this model (trial of strength) and in the direction of a trial of *wills*. The meaning of the distinction is this: what becomes crucial in a nuclear confrontation is the *will* to use weapons which both sides know are capable of wreaking havoc far in excess of any rational policy. It is by threatening to abandon rationality altogether that each side hopes to frighten the other into moderation. If this threat is serious, and it *must* be for it to work, then we abandon altogether any possibility of employing force with discrimination and proportionality and any possibility of employing force as a means to some moral or political end.

A nation determined to play a game of wills to the end, and resolved to will in accord with the internal "rationality" of a radical voluntarism, never will discover that there are any limits in resolutely willing to win this game of hostile wills in conflict. Not here is to be found any *ratio* in the *ultima ratio* of the arbitrament of arms. A nation comes upon no boundaries in this upward spiral, so long as proper acts of war are believed to arise but out of contending wills. Unfortunately, in this, a commander can show his resolution in no other way than by proving that he is willing to sacrifice one or more of his own cities; and he must reduce the enemy's cities to rubble as a means of getting at his resolution. This is the very definition of the unjust conduct of war.[2]

One objection to the concept of massive retaliation, then, is that it divorces force from rational choice; the more limited are our options, the more credible is the deterrent threat. Ideally, massive retaliation as a deterrent would be maximized by eliminating choice altogether. This was precisely the point of Herman Khan's famous proposal for a "doomsday machine," consisting of a number of nuclear devices wired together in such a way that if they are detonated the entire world will be destroyed. Potential enemies are, of course, informed of the existence of the machine and of the fact that any intrusion by nuclear weapons into the territory of the country which owns the machine will trigger it. As a necessary added feature, the builders set the machine in such a way that any attempt to disconnect it will result in its detonation. Thus, once set in operation, no one can turn off the machine, including its creators. The purpose of such an instrument is to remove conclusively from the minds of any potential enemy any doubts they might have about the weakness of our will or any other "human" element which might play a part in their war calculations. We are, in effect, saying to them that we have opted out of the realm of rational choice and control over the employment of nuclear weapons in order to insure that the enemy does not miscalculate on the basis of what he judges are our intentions. Under the circumstances we no longer have any relevant intentions.

When Khan first made his proposal he was, and still is, widely misunderstood. Critics supposed that he was actually recommending construction of the device. In fact, Khan was only pointing out that once we accept the "rationality of the irrational" we are logically committed to the doomsday machine. For if war is a contest of will only, then we are required to "set" our will in such a manner that there will be no question of our not following through. The doomsday machine represents a way of doing this, and the huge outcry against Khan is evidence of the dawning realization of precisely what is entailed by war so conceived.

Since the idea of morality is intimately connected with the possibility of human agency, any weapons system which restricts or eliminates choice is morally undesirable. But the same is true of politics: to limit choice is to reduce options for the policy maker. Because massive retaliation depends upon a willingness to be irrational, "rationality" demands a retreat from choice and thus makes a mockery of both morals and statecraft.

In addition to this matter of war becoming a contest of

wills, there is the second defect referred to earlier. As with saturation bombing, it is simply not plausible to regard noncombatant deaths as collateral damage, and this for two reasons. First, under the theory of massive retaliation it is *cities themselves* which are targeted. Noncombatants are the direct objects of attack under this plan; their vulnerability to attack will supposedly ensure that war is avoided. But to *threaten* direct attack upon noncombatants is also immoral and, indeed, is a form of terrorism. Second, even if one attempts to justify massive retaliation in terms of conventional military necessity, as Truman did in the Hiroshima bombing, the attempt is implausible given the essentially indiscriminate character of the weapon and the fact that alternative, discriminate weapons are available.

The staringly obvious moral and prudential objections to massive retaliation were finally felt by the middle of the 1960s. In a speech now famous, then Secretary of Defense Robert MacNamara proposed to the Soviets that both sides shift from a countervalue to a counterforce nuclear strategy. These terms are part of the jargon of modern strategic thinking, and they refer to attacks upon noncombatants and upon combatants, respectively. The Soviets were invited to join the Americans and others in removing all missile silos and other combat paraphernalia from population centers. The rationale for such a proposal is that if total nuclear disarmament is impossible (and we will assume for now that it is), then the only morally acceptable alternative is some form of counterforce strike capability directed toward the enemy's missiles and other armed forces, avoiding his populated areas. Counterforce exchanges would supposedly avoid wholly disproportionate noncombatant damage and, thereby, restore war to a trial of strength. Such a strategy presupposes that both sides will cooperate in the construction of their missile silos and the emplacement of their armies in areas sufficiently remote from civilian centers.

The proposal to shift to counterforce has been widely supported by defenders of *bellum justum*. In the first place, it seems to afford a means of returning warfare to a trial of strength—our missiles are being fired at other missiles and at combatants. If combat is thus restricted, there can be no question of a continuing escalation of the sort associated with a trial of wills. Thus the requirements of discrimination and proportionality are satisfied, in that we can now plausibly be said to be directing force against combatants and to be seeking to avoid damage disproportionate to the ends being sought by the war. In short, counterforce appears to be a proposal within the tradition of restraining force.

I regret to say that I do not believe the foregoing argument will work. In saying this, I also believe that it is important to understand the dilemma in which many defenders of *bellum justum* find themselves: If, as many suppose, nuclear weapons are a permanent feature of international life, then even though we know that their employment would result in damage disproportionate to any moral end, we are obliged to do what we can to minimize the killing. If counterforce will save *some* lives, if these terrible weapons can be even moderately "restrained," this is better than taking an unrealistic prohibitionist position. I believe we must reject the "lesser of two evils" argument in the case of nuclear weapons for essentially three reasons:

First, even if counterforce were seriously subscribed to by both sides, the weapons themselves remain *essentially* indiscriminate; they remain potentially countervalue. With weapons of this destructive power we are at an altogether novel conceptual level. To possess the power to kill all living things on earth in a matter of minutes is not to possess power merely in a larger degree than in times past. For as there is no real defense against nuclear weapons massively deployed, we cannot but see the mere possession of them as coercive in a way which has no historical precedent.

Second, suppose that the counterforce proposal were accompanied by an agreement to deploy only *tactical* nuclear weapons: this would still, I fear, be unsatisfactory. The problem with nuclear weapons is their potential for utter destruction; they are a *type* of weapon wholly unacceptable, no matter what the immediate destructive capacity. On this basis we ought to oppose the use of any nuclear weapons whatever, because what is absolutely crucial is the crossing of the nuclear threshold at all. Once that is done, at however modest a level, we tacitly accept the technology of countervalue; we "plug in" to the technology of total destruction.

Third, even if it were possible to overcome these first two objections in some way, counterforce would only work in states with very large territories, such as the Soviet Union, China, and the United States. What would counterforce mean for small states such as Britain and France, an objection temporarily and partially answered by nuclear submarines?

The claim that nuclear weapons are in some way *essentially* different from conventional arms and, therefore, that the very possession of them is immoral, will strike some critics as simply false. What, for example, would mark the distinction between atomic bombs and incendiary bombs of the sort dropped on Japan with such devastating effect prior to the attack on Hiroshima? Both of these indiscriminate attacks produced identical effects (with the exception of radiation damage). Such an objection seems plausible — nuclear weapons are perhaps easier to deliver, requiring only a single plane or missile instead of the many dozens of aircraft used in a conventional raid; but that is the only significant difference. There is no *special* moral problem about nuclear weapons.

We understand this objection, and yet there has, from the beginning, been deep moral controversy and unease over nuclear weapons. Starting with the initial moral disputes among those building the atomic bomb, continuing through the controversy surrounding its use against the Japanese, through the agitation to "Ban the Bomb" during the 1950s, and down to present efforts to limit nuclear weapons, there has been a persistent argument that nuclear weapons should be completely eliminated.

There are, it seems to me, two ways of articulating the intuition that nuclear weapons are "different" from conventional weapons. For one, any object which can be described as a weapon has the potential for misuse. A stone or a length of wood can be used to commit murder, but either one can also be used with discrimination, as when a policeman incapacitates an assailant with his truncheon. The history of weaponry doubtless suggests a movement in the direction of the ever-greater possibility of doing indiscriminate violence (although there are some interesting exceptions). It remains the case, however, that the current conventional weapons inventory of modern armies has the possibility of discriminate and proportionate employment. Historically, weapons which are indiscriminate in themselves or which cannot be used discriminately because of delivery problems have generally been abandoned or proscribed. Poison gas and bacteriological warfare come to mind. These might be delivered in sufficiently small quantities to satisfy discrimination and proportionality, but it was discovered fairly early on that such substances as gas and microbes are extremely hard to control. Gas, for example, is subject to the vagaries of wind and weather; a sudden change in wind direction can return the gas whence it came; rain can destroy its effectiveness. Gas can also linger in areas for long periods of time, thus hampering attack and occupation of enemy territory. So, in cases where particular weapons cannot be used because we lack the means to deliver or control them in a discriminate way (or in a way which is not self-defeating) or where the weapon seems to have an *intended* disproportionate effect upon combatants, as with the dumdum bullet, these have generally fallen from use or have been banned. There are a number of modern exceptions (the Stoner rifle, whose bullet duplicates the damage of the old dumdum, is one example), but these exceptions are singled out for moral controversy. Moreover, certain weapons which have been problematic in the past, such as conventional air bombardment and artillery, can now be delivered with an extraordinary degree of precision, for example, radar-controlled artillery, so-called smart bombs which are targeted by laser beams, heat-seeking air-to-ground missiles for use against armor, and so on. So that while air bombardment reached the ultimate in lack of discrimination about 1940, it has been getting more precise ever since. Aircraft can now pinpoint a very small target, such as a bridge or a house, from a great height. This is a good example of the *reversal* of a trend toward more indiscriminate weapons.

Thus, while the inventory of modern conventional weapons can be misused in various ways, they *can* also be used with discrimination and proportionality. The same is not the case with the atomic and hydrogen bombs which constitute the deterrent force of the nuclear powers. These weapons, if used, cannot but be misused. A nuclear attack, except in extremely remote areas such as outer space, will necessarily be indiscriminate and disproportionate. Also, because of fallout and nuclear contamination, secondary indiscriminate damage is likely.

To possess atomic and hydrogen bombs as part of a deterrence system is a standing threat to noncombatants in a way that the possession of conventional weapons is not, for the latter *can* be used justly, the former can be used *only* unjustly. Nuclear deterrence is, therefore, quite unlike earlier forms of conventional deterrence such as the Royal Navy's policy of having a fleet as large as any two combined fleets.

It might be objected against what I have said that it is not, in fact, immoral to *threaten* to use nuclear weapons if such threats might actually deter others from aggressive war and if such threats were "empty." That is, as long as we merely threaten to use nuclear weapons while affirming to ourselves the commitment never to actually use them, no harm is done and the possible deterrent effect is achieved. Thus, our outward posture may be bellicose, but we say to ourselves (as it were) that we will never use the weapons, even if attacked. For if we are attacked with nuclear weapons, deterrence will have failed anyway.

The question of *intention* has been much debated in the literature on war and ethics. It is often alleged that it is not only immoral to employ such weapons but that even to possess and threaten to use them is immoral as well. There are various points to be carefully distinguished here.

Bluff. One way out of this dilemma would be to possess nuclear weapons but never intend to use them. This would amount to a policy of bluff. We would act as if we were fully committed to a policy of deterrence, but if we were actually attacked, we would not retaliate, on the grounds that as deterrence had failed, our response would be merely revenge. Nothing of political or moral significance would be accomplished by launching at this stage. There are serious problems with this argument. When we speak of "bluff," whose intentions are we talking about? While the President of the United States might well make a personal decision to refuse to launch these weapons, there is no way to bind his successors to such an agreement (or, indeed, even to guarantee that he would not have a change of heart himself). Even if this difficulty could somehow be overcome, military personnel down the chain of command are most certainly not bluffing. They are necessarily trained to respond to direct orders from above, so that *their* intentions are clear. Now, at least some of these people possess independent launch capability. Although there are safeguards built into the system, it is possible for several officers in collusion to effect an independent launch. Therefore, it seems obvious that while bluff might be the personal decision of a particular national leader, it could never be a *national* policy.

To take this a step further, it would probably make no difference whatever if tomorrow the president publicly stated that the United States would under no circumstances ever use nuclear weapons. Why should potential enemies believe him? How could he make this kind of absolutist policy binding upon his successors, or even upon himself in future years?

Conditional intentions.   A policy of bluff must be distinguished from one of conditional intention. In this latter case, we express an intention to do *x* if condition *y* obtains, when we have not fully decided what we *would* do if *y* happened. This seems to more accurately describe our real situation. It is our stated intention to retaliate if the Soviets attack with nuclear weapons without, I think, knowing for certain whether we would in fact retaliate in such an eventuality. Indeed, it might be argued that "keeping the Russians guessing" about our intentions is a more attractive form of deterrence than if they knew for certain what we would do.

It is sometimes said that mere possession of nuclear weapons is not in itself immoral. A homeowner can surely display a weapon openly in order to deter intruders without ever intending to use it. This may be granted, but there is, in addition to what I have said about "bluff" being an impossible national policy, an important difference between this case and nuclear deterrence. The United States and the Soviet Union have a policy of targeting each other's countries on a twenty-four-hour basis. Our weapons are not simply stored somewhere but are part of a strategy of implementation. Both sides are, therefore, encouraged to expect that the other side *will* use these weapons.

Counterforce.   It is sometimes claimed that counterforce strategy undercuts the whole problem of intention, in virtue of the fact that we do not target the Soviet population as such. We are not interested, that is, in killing Soviet citizens but in destroying their capacity to fight back. In pursuit of this we target their missile silos, military bases, industrial production, communications, and so forth. This is true but morally irrelevant. There are fourteen thousand targets in the Soviet Union; sixty of them are in Moscow. Whether or not we "intend" to kill noncombatants, such destruction would clearly violate the principle of proportionality. In this case, we can hardly fall back on the principle of double effect.

To repeat, the problem is not so much intention as the weapon itself, which if used in its present strategy of preparedness, can be used only immorally. To threaten to use nuclear weapons is necessarily to threaten the unjustified killing of innocent people and thereby to violate on a titanic scale the absolute right of life.

In short, because of the real possibility of total destruction or damage quite beyond the realm of any conceivable moral or political requirement, there is no way to "save" nuclear weapons, even tactical nuclear weapons. Defenders of *bellum justum* ought to face up to this and realize that, for once, there is no accommodation possible with a weapons system of this sort; nuclear weapons represent not just another run up the ladder from conventional bombing but a different ladder altogether.

What, then, does this entail about disarmament? If nuclear weapons are totally unacceptable, then should we not give them up, unilaterally, if necessary? It is interesting to see Walzer wrestle with this question. Characteristically, he assigns the problem to "supreme emergency," though what the "emergency" is he does not say. What is the "absolute evil" which we are forestalling by retaining nuclear weapons? I believe that Walzer is even more unsatisfactory here than in his account of noncombatant immunity.

I should like to argue that unilateral disarmament is not morally required (though reasonable persons might disagree on this), because deterrence essentially represents a *balance*. A unilateral shift toward imbalance might destabilize the situation and create the outcome which this form of disarmament tries to avoid. Nuclear weapons cannot be un-invented. They are like a dreadful bacillus which we cannot destroy but can only innoculate ourselves against. Deterrence represents one way to stabilize the situation, but it is extremely dangerous and morally risky. Unilateral disarmament is, in my view, equally so. What is required here is arms control, though the history of such negotiations is not encouraging.

Another major difficulty is the attitude of the Soviet Union toward deterrence. They are required to participate in the strategy of counterforce targeting, but their attitude toward deterrence differs in important respects from that of the West. The Soviets do not regard their nuclear stockpile as anything but another weapons system in their arsenal, one which they are quite prepared (they say) to use if their homeland is invaded. Thus, if nuclear weapons have to be used, the Soviets do not necessarily mark this down as failure. After all, they lost twenty million lives in the war against Hitler and suffered devastation of their physical resources equivalent to a small-scale nuclear war. Thus, from their point of view, twenty million killed is at least the "ante" in any future war.

The Soviet attitude raises a more fundamental ethical question. Let us say that the crusade in World War II to eliminate the threat of Hitler resulted in sixty million dead (many of them civilians). Suppose in 1939 we had known that this would be the cost. Would it have made a difference in our resolution? In hindsight, would anyone care to say that the destruction of Nazi power was not worth the killing? If we are *not* prepared to say this, then can we avoid the conclusion that sixty million dead, accompanied by incredible devastation, is not *our* ante—the minimal price we are prepared to pay to counter any future threat equivalent to Hitler?

Whatever the answers to these questions may be, it is obvious that *no* interests, political or moral, are served by a nuclear war between the Soviet Union and the United States and that the survival of the race is at issue.

The dilemma, as I see it, is that we have no choice but to rely on deterrence (as nuclear weapons will always be with us) but that deterrence is becoming increasingly risky. Apologists for deterrence are prone to say that deterrence has "worked" for the past forty years and that is a strong argument for its continuation. But this would be a good argument only if the delivery systems and the destructive power of nuclear weapons had remained constant. This has obviously not been the case. The launch-target time of delivery systems has radically decreased over the years, so that now there is a talk of satellite-launched missiles which will reach their targets in 280 seconds. Under these conditions it will be necessary to rely totally on computer-programmed responses. When that happens, all human control and choice about the fate of mankind will be eliminated; accident and error will find no forgiveness in the face of computer responses. It is obvious that we have here gone beyond war to the level of a suicide pact. Any negotiations, therefore, should aim at decreasing the *risks* of deterrence, not at eliminating it.

One final point: Whatever minimal moral credibility our possession of nuclear weapons retains depends strictly on their *exclusive* deployment to deter the nuclear weapons of the Soviet Union. If they are used for any lesser role (such as the prevention of a conventional attack on Western Europe), then the threat will be wholly disproportionate to the goal.

To turn now to the question of irregular warfare, one widely held point of view on the cause of insurgency claims that this form of warfare has developed in response to the impasse created by massive retaliation. It is because nations find that they can no longer meet in a direct confrontation with each other that they have chosen to meet indirectly in Third-World guerrilla wars. In this sense, the insurgents are surrogates for the great powers, fighting wars which their masters cannot risk doing openly. An alternative conception of insurgency sees the guerrilla as the spearpoint of the revolution of oppressed peoples the world over. These views are in no way incompatible, nor do they exclude less cosmic causes such as internal or local disputes or even banditry. Because guerrilla war is so unstructured, all sorts of "guerrillas" from idealogue to criminal may be expected to join the fighting.

The peculiar difficulties which just war thinking encounters here are the same as those we met with in our discussion of nuclear war. Because the insurgent has such a close relation with the populace, and because he does not fight in conventional terms, there is the danger that the target may be enlarged to include noncombatants. Moreover, as the guerrilla typically cannot hope to defeat the enemy forces in the field, he will be forced into a war of attrition. His target becomes the enemy's will and not his forces. Thus by grinding down the will of the enemy, he hopes to win a victory which is essentially political: without defeating the military forces of the enemy, he wishes simply to prolong the struggle until his opponent's will to continue the struggle is broken.

It is important at the outset to draw a distinction between terrorism and guerrilla warfare, as the two are frequently falsely equated. As we have observed, terrorism may be a feature of conventional war. It is certainly not a necessary feature of guerrilla war in theory or in practice. The doyen of guerrilla warriors, Mao Zedong, explicitly rejected it on the grounds that the task of the guerrilla is to be the vanguard of the people and that terrorism should simply alienate them, so that guerrilla warfare ought to involve the *least* amount of terrorism of any form of warfare. There are, however, a large number of activists who claim that terror is justified, and they generally support, as its vehicle, some type of insurgency. There are basically two forms which the defense takes. The first we have already discussed in connection with the Margolis quotation, but I will give one further example of it. These are the words of George Habbash, of the Popular Front for the Liberation of Palestine: "In the age of the revolution of peoples oppressed by the world imperialist system there can be no geographical or political boundaries or moral limits to the operations of the people's camp. In today's world no one is 'innocent,' and

no one is a 'neutral.'"³ What this in effect claims is that
there is no such thing as terrorism anymore, since "terrorism" can only be defined in terms of a distinction between combatants and noncombatants, a distinction which
no longer obtains; if no one is "innocent," then everyone
is fair game. We have already discussed the implausibility
of this view. I will only add that the activities of Habbash
and his colleagues speak for themselves.

The second, and more interesting, line of argument in
support of terrorism is based upon a kind of utilitarian
calculus. Robert Taber, discussing an incident in the Mo-
roccan insurgency, puts it this way:

> The ultimate cost was nevertheless far lighter than it would have
> been, the terror more merciful (if that is the word) than any cam-
> paign of what we choose to call *conventional war*.
> The reason is clear. In Morocco, as in Israel and Ireland, re-
> volutionary warfare provided a shortcut; the pressure generated
> by terrorism and political agitation proved more potent than in-
> fantry divisions and aircraft.⁴

These sentiments are, of course, completely at odds with
traditional just-war doctrine. Direct attacks upon noncombatants as a means of effecting political change are the very
essence of unjust conduct in war. The reasons for this are
fairly straightforward. First, from the moral point of view it
is not possible for one rationally to will that terrorism should
become a universal law, applicable to oneself. This would
entail an individual willing that he ought himself to be
made the object of a direct attack even if he were a noncombatant. It would also entail his willing that his children
should also be so treated, not to mention that children in
general should be declared rightful objects of attack. Thus
terrorism can never become a *moral* principle.

From the prudential point of view it is not in the interests
of states that any form of indiscriminate warfare become
officially acceptable. War, we have argued, is a political
act, and as such it must be directed to the production of
concrete goals. States have discovered that the best means

of doing this is to create a class of uniformed combatants who will resolve outstanding issues by a trial of strength. Historically, any attempt to short-circuit this procedure has been disastrous. The justice and urgency of one's own cause may easily tempt one to take the shortcut, but the long-range consequences of doing so are uniformly imprudent, for once the "shortcut" is established as precedent, then nothing is easier than for one's opponents to imitate it. As Liddell-Hart has perceptively demonstrated, the eagerness with which the Allies fomented irregular war during World War II has been imitated and turned against them, often in the very areas where they first introduced such tactics.* And Taber is wrong on another point. Terrorism tends to be ineffectual as a shortcut precisely because it involves attacks upon noncombatants, thereby creating a climate of fear and hatred which tends to linger on indefinitely. Two of the countries Taber mentions are actually counterexamples to his thesis: Israel and Ireland. The sad history of those two countries is directly connected with the practice of terrorism. How often do the P.L.O. justify their own acts of terror by pointing to Prime Minister Begin's participation in the massacre at Dir Yasin?

But even their [terrorist] achievements are often problematical. By aggravating the crisis, they make the solution of the problem more difficult or even impossible. For national and religious minorities are dispersed in such a way in today's world that resolving one grievance usually creates a new one. Given the complexity of the modern world, not every minority can have a state of its own. Seemingly successful terrorist operations (such as in Cyprus) have, in fact, ended in disaster insofar as they have poisoned the relations between the communities and made peaceful co-existence impossible. Recent events in Ulster and the Middle East may have the same results: The longer terrorism lasts, the stronger the belief that there will be no peace until the other group is annihilated. With the progress in terrorist technology from the dagger to the means of mass destruction, the consequences seem ominous.[5]

*See Appendix.

The main point about terrorism is this: Every political community has understood that random and indiscriminate violence is the ultimate threat to social cohesion, and thus every political community has some form of prohibition against it. Terrorism allowed full sway would reduce civil society to the state of nature where there is, in Hobbes's fine description, "continual fear of violet death, and the life of man, poor, nasty, brutish and short." No political society can sanction terrorism, for that would be a self-contradiction, as the very reasons for entering civil society were to escape precisely those conditions imposed by the terrorist. This is why a little judicious terrorism is not really possible, for the fear it engenders and the precedent it sets will most certainly outweigh any "moral value" it might have as a shortcut. This, incidentally, reveals once again the poverty of a certain utilitarian model that treats human lives as identical counters in a bargaining game; it matters a great deal, morally, what kinds of lives are taken and by what means.

Turning back to the question of guerrilla warfare, we can now distinguish that form of conflict from terrorism as such. It is in principle possible to fight a guerrilla war without making direct attacks upon noncombatants. As we have seen, the guerrilla depends upon the support of the populace much more intimately than a conventional soldier, and so he may be expected to be especially careful in his behavior toward them.

The moral problems caused by insurgency warfare are created by two facts. First, conventional armies are psychologically and materially set up to fight against a clearly defined group of enemy combatants. In this sense, insurgents are in violation of the rules of war governing the conduct of belligerents—for example, the requirement of having "a fixed distinctive emblem recognizable at a distance, the carrying of arms openly, and generally conducting operations in accordance with the laws and customs of war." Second, conventional armies are also psychologically "set" (as is the population back home) to expect war to consist of a series of battles covering a reasonably short span of time and culminating in a military victory. The insurgent violates these expectations by refusing battle in the conventional sense in favor of continual and wearing "pin-prick" pressures and by prolonging the conflict in the hope of tiring the enemy. When these expectations are frustrated, conventional soldiers take shortcuts.

Let us look at these two points in order. Insurgency is thought to involve a special problem because of the putative identification of the guerrilla with the populace. This relationship is given classic expression by Mao Zedong. According to Mao, guerrilla war develops in three stages. In the first stage the insurgent forces, which are likely to be small in number, engage in hit-and-run encounters with regular forces. In this way they draw attention to their cause and increase their supply of arms and equipment (captured from the regular forces). These opening guns pave the way for the second stage, which consists of building a political infrastructure which will parallel that of the government in power. This creates a country within a country and is a necessary move toward the third stage, which sees the insurgents emerging openly in order to do battle with the army of the government in a more or less conventional manner.

According to standard doctrine, it is essential to prevent an insurgent movement from getting beyond the first stage. Once an alternative political order comes into being, the task of the counterinsurgent is doubled, for he has now to combat the military forces of the insurgency as well as their political structures. Furthermore, the mass of the people are no longer forced to rely exclusively upon the government for social and political services, rudimentary as these may have been in any case. From the insurgents' point of view, it is necessary that they accomplish the second stage as rapidly as possible in order to distinguish themselves from mere bandits.

The necessity of nipping insurgency in the bud creates

a number of problems for the intervening power, not the least of which is the technical problem of getting sufficient force into the host country at short notice. A moral dilemma is created, on the one hand, by the demand for rapid deployment in order to prevent a long and costly war with its suffering and destruction and, on the other hand, by the twin demands of the rules of war concerning the intervention of one nation in the affairs of others and the necessity of possessing a clear political goal for intervention. The intervening power will often be torn between the requirement for haste and the relative lack of conventional criteria which would justify the use of force. Given currently accepted doctrines about when war is and is not justified, guerrilla warfare fails to exhibit some of the more notable features which count as sufficient conditions for going to war. For example, the outright invasion of an independent country with which we have defensive alliances is normally regarded as a situation adequate to activate our alliance. Sending troops across the borders of a sovereign state is prima facie evidence of aggression, and, as such, the aggressor is a candidate for condemnation by the community of nations. The United Nations action in Korea and the censure by that body of Britain, France, and Israel for the invasion of Egypt in 1956 exemplify this principle.

Insurgency need not, of course, involve troops across borders. One country may foment insurgency in another even though they do not share a common boundary. The lengthy and inconclusive debates over whether South Vietnam was or was not being invaded by North Vietnam reflect the uneasiness which the intervening power feels in not clearly having satisfied the troops-across-border criterion. Another classic example is the fact that the United Nations, the Organization of American States, and the Rio Pact were unable to take action over the Cuban insurgency.

Thus, rapid deployment runs a clear risk. If the threat of insurgency turns out to have been exaggerated, the intervening power is open to the charge of imperialism. If the insurgency is the beginning of a genuine civil war between purely nationalist factions, the intervening power may well be castigated for interfering in the internal affairs of a sovereign state, risking confrontation with the major powers, and so forth. This will likely occur even if the intervention is invited by one of the factions. For one of the most difficult problems in counterinsurgency is the determination of which (if any) of the many contending forces *is* the government. To justify intervention on the grounds that the "government invited us in" will, in some cases, be to beg the question.

The conclusion here seems to be that problems of intervention are greatly exacerbated by the lack of conventional criteria for determining aggression. This is of great importance, because self-defense, or resistance to aggression, is the only justification which the modern interpretation of *bellum justum* and international law will allow for the resort to war. When we add to this the necessity for rapid deployment, the counterinsurgent is at the outset in a markedly inferior position. Moreover, owing to the requirement of halting insurgency before it gets out of the early stage, the intervening power may find that it is forced to ally itself with host country regimes which it finds morally repulsive:

One fact of life emerges. The less the justification, the quicker the successful action must be. There is no doubt that if victory in Vietnam had been achieved by 1963 there would have been resounding applause all around, and even if achieved in 1966, after the commitment of the United States forces and the bombing of the North, little harm would have been done and most criticism would have been stilled. The longer the period and the larger the scale of the involvement are likely to be, the better must be the cause if damage to grand strategy is to be avoided. This all leads to the awkward conclusion that it is better to back a quick winner who may be wrong than a slow loser who may be right.[6]

The moral problems surrounding intervention quickly pale, however, in comparison with difficulties encountered in the fighting. As we have noted, guerrilla warfare tends to blur the distinction between combatant and noncombatant, and to the extent that it does so, culpability for noncombatant deaths will rest with the guerrillas who initiated this mode of fighting. Consider this example:

In Vietnam children are trained for weeks, sometimes for months, to walk with equally spaced steps. Then one day they are sent to an American base to shine shoes. They walk and count the distances between each shed, each store of weapons and each sandbag embankment.

The women who wash the G.I.'s laundry also walk with an equal step and count the steps that separate a command post and the guard defending it. The information is sent to the city, where other people meticulously collate it and eventually draw up a complete plan of the base. It is sent off into the jungle where it is turned into an exact model in which commandos will train for weeks or even months, and then one day there will be an attack in which nothing is left to chance.[7]

In a case such as this the guerrilla must bear a heavy share of guilt for using children and other noncombatants in this way. However, this obviously does not entail permission for the counterinsurgent to employ whatever means he likes in whatever proportion. He will still be under obligation to follow the rules of war. Thus, the alleged dilemma: given the close identification of guerrillas with the populace (summarized in Mao's aphorism, "The guerrilla is the fish and the people are the water in which the fish swims"), such warfare is *essentially* indiscriminate, so that we either do not fight or we fight and the rules of war are ignored.

The choice between surrender and ignoring the rules of war is bogus. The dilemma is possible only because counterinsurgents have attempted to employ conventional forces using conventional tactics in a situation requiring something very different. Instead of looking upon the insurgent as a combatant unfairly disguising himself as a noncombatant, it is preferable to describe him on the analogy of the criminal. There is a much greater similarity between the guerrilla and the ordinary criminal than there is between the guerrilla and the soldier. Consider their points of similarity: Neither one wears a uniform, thus no doubt making the job of the policeman much more difficult. Similarly, neither carries arms openly or has a distinct emblem visible at a distance, as is required by the rules of war. They both live and move within the civil populace, in some cases even aided by that populace. Both of them refrain from engaging in full-scale conventional battles but operate indirectly and at random. In spite of all these disadvantages, the operations of the police are much more highly regulated than those of the soldier. One cannot imagine a policeman uttering those immortal words spoken by an American colonel in Vietnam: "In order to save this village from the guerrillas, we had to destroy it." What is the difference between the generally discriminate and proportional use of force by police against criminals and the alleged indiscriminate and disproportionate use of force by soldiers fighting guerrillas? In a word: intelligence. The gathering of information and evidence is a crucial activity of police as a prelude to the use of force. This is in order to make absolutely certain that if force is necessary, it is directed toward the criminal and no one else. And, of course, the policeman, like the soldier, uses force with the intent to restrain or incapacitate. What I am saying is that counterinsurgency must be perceived as a constabulary operation rather than an act of warfare in the traditional sense. This is required for two reasons. First, no other method will be militarily effective. The consensus about Vietnam in this postmortem period is that the United States forces consistently lacked the kind of intelligence which would have enabled them to pinpoint guerrilla strongholds and to identify Viet Cong personnel, particularly the leaders of the village cells. This meant that American forces were operating "blind," hence the overreliance on hardware and sheer weight of metal. Second, lack of intelligence creates the conditions for an immoral use of force in an insurgency situation. The counterinsurgent will inevitably find himself making mistakes in his use of firepower; and as his frustration at not being able to pinpoint the enemy increases, so does the likelihood of direct attacks upon noncombatants.

The war in Vietnam will stand as the classic example of how not to fight insurgents. What Vietnam proved was not that the rules of war were outmoded by guerrilla warfare but that conventional armies using conventional tactics cannot achieve military success or moral respectability against insurgents. In particular, the American failure may be attributed to three factors. The first was racism. For the average American the Vietnamese were a mass of indistinguishable individuals with a way of life which was simultaneously inexplicable and repulsive. Under these circumstances the gathering of intelligence, the lifeblood of counterinsurgency, was stifled and the war lost from the very beginning. The second factor concerned hardware and conventional tactics. The American reliance on artillery and air strikes at the expense of small unit tactics was not only indiscriminate but served to forewarn the Viet Cong of the exact location of the proposed engagement so that they could escape or engage as suited them. The third factor was conscription. Just as one requires a professional police force to combat crime effectively and morally, so one requires a professional, long-term counterinsurgency force. Such a force will not be effectively formed from conscripts. The point I want to stress is that while insurgency does create problems for the just conduct of war, they are not intractable provided the insurgents do not engage in terrorism and provided the counterinsurgents conceive of their task as essentially constabulary.

It might be argued that guerrilla warfare conceived on the analogy of police work breaks down. In the case of ordinary police work, it may be argued, the authorities have the support of the populace; criminals are perceived by citizens to be a threat. I will fully grant that, unless the populace supports, in a general way, the activities of counterinsurgents, there is no hope of success. But then a counterinsurgency which lacks popular support is doomed in any case. What can be said is that history has shown that any spirit of cooperation between civil and military authorities is quickly extinguished by the indiscriminate use of force characteristic of conventional armies fighting guerrillas. So *if* counterinsurgency is possible, its chances for success, tactically and morally, are greater if it is carried out by a force trained on the constabulary model.

The second major problem with guerrilla warfare is not so much moral as psychological. Wars of attrition generally come down to a struggle of will. We have noted that just-war thinking has usually opposed conflicts of will on the twofold grounds that war is prolonged and often removed from rational control. In fighting an enemy whose tactic is attrition, these factors must be kept to the fore. Unfortunately, attrition runs counter to the prevailing view of war in the West. Both the popular and official government expectations of the Western democracies are that wars will be just, that they will be brief, and that they will conclude in victory for the democracies. Since justice is currently equated with opposing aggression, our view of war tends to take on the character of a brief but successful crusade against evil. In this context, the concept of victory comes to be perceived as an *event,* which is achieved on the field of combat by means of the "big push," the "last battle," or the "unconditional surrender." But as the insurgent's concern is with a political solution, he refuses to play a role in this scenario. For him the major part of the struggle is the gradual grinding down of the will of the enemy to go on fighting. As Mao Zedong's historical mentor Sun Tzu put it:

There is no art higher than that of destroying the enemy's resistance on the battlefield. Spread disunity and dispute among the citizens of the enemy's country. Turn the young against the old. Use every means to destroy their arms, their supplies and the discipline of the enemy's forces. Debase old traditions and accepted gods.[8]

Guerrilla tactics are equally indirect. Che Guevara describes a movement called the "minuet," which consists of hitting the enemy from four sides and then melting away, only to return later in order to renew pressure on the van of the marching column.[9] Such repeated hit-and-run tactics have the effect of sowing fear in the remainder of the formation. The insurgent's prime target is the will of the enemy, and he is, therefore, unconcerned with scoring "wins" in a conventional military sense. Furthermore, because he sees himself as the vanguard of the people and not as a force raised for a specific time and mission, he is independent of timetables. Unless the intervening power has established a bipartisan counterinsurgency policy, its commitment may have to be altered in four or five years. Needless to say, insurgents are fully aware of this kind of potential weakness.

The Western concept of war, neatly summarized in Tawney's aphorism "War is either a crusade or it is a crime," has the practical consequence of making the armed forces instrumentalities raised for specific, relatively short-run objectives. The Western maxim "Keep politics out of the army and the army out of politics" stands in total opposition to the doctrine of insurgency. The soldier is the fish and the people are the water. This explains the consistent lack of success which Western-style armies have experienced in bringing guerrilla forces to the decisive battle. In these circumstances there is no "decisive battle," nor is there anything corresponding to victory in the ordinary sense—although it should not be supposed that there is nothing corresponding to the traditional concept of defeat.

As noted earlier, there is no direct connection between terrorism and guerrilla war; in fact, guerrillas must take special care not to antagonize the civil populace upon whom they depend for food, shelter, and moral support. There is, however, an indirect connection between guerrilla war and terrorism: the guerrilla has no need to practice terrorism, for he can get the counterinsurgents to do it for him. By failing to clearly distinguish himself from the civil population, he draws the (usually devastating) fire of the counterinsurgent upon them. It seems clear that this is intentional on the part of the guerrilla or, at the very least, not unwelcome to him. Because *he* does not directly cause the death of civilians, he can claim that his opponents are behaving indiscriminately. In other words, the success of guerrilla warfare presupposes *jus in bello* and, especially, the principle of noncombatant immunity. Because the guerrilla can, typically, count on his opponents to respect the immunity of civilians, his position is greatly reinforced in two ways.

First, because he knows that the counterinsurgent will adhere to *jus in bello,* he can withdraw when it suits him to the relative safety of the civilian sector. By "becoming" a civilian, the guerrilla is thus able to decide when and where he will fight and when and where he will be a target for attack. The counterinsurgent is *always* fair game because always a combatant.

Second, inevitably, in the attempt to separate the guerrillas from the civilians, some of the latter will be killed. This may be a tactic of the guerrilla: Act so as to draw the fire of the counterinsurgent upon civilians, then say to them and to the world, "Behold the slaughter of the innocents." The counterinsurgent will argue that the guerrilla has created these conditions, but the deed will have been done, and world opinion will register only the fact of dead women and children.

The guerrilla is responsible for noncombatant deaths caused by his deliberate identification with them. He takes advantage of the moral outrage engendered when soldiers attack civilians. The guerrilla is involved here in a double moral error: not only is he using civilians as mere means, but he is also relying upon the principle of noncombatant immunity while acting in such a way as to undermine it.

All of this suggests the necessity of making explicit a presupposition of *jus in bello,* one which is frequently not made clear. I have argued that the justified use of force entails that (all things being equal) violence will be the province of a special class of combatants. Only if this condition is satisfied can our moral beliefs about the value of other persons, as well as our prudential concerns about unleashing violence, also be satisfied. If we are to arm soldiers and give them permission to do violence, then we must protect civilians from them. This is why the principle of noncombatant immunity is of such importance and why I have devoted so much space to discussing it. There is still another side to this issue. If civilians must be protected from soldiers, then it follows that soldiers must also be protected from civilians. We require, that is, a principle of "combatant immunity." Soldiers must be guaranteed against attack from the civilian quarter if they are to carry out their duties as combatants and if they are to respect the immunity of civilians. Soldiers *and* civilians can be murdered.

The guerrilla violates the principle of combatant immunity when he takes on the guise of a civilian, and he, therefore, becomes a threat to noncombatants because he undermines the principle which protects them. This in turn weakens *jus in bello* and, ultimately, our attempts to provide moral justification for restrained force. Thus guerrilla warfare seems to contain the same moral defect which we saw in nuclear weapons, that is, as a *form* of warfare it depends for its effectiveness upon some form of terrorism. In the case of guerrilla warfare this generalization admits of some exceptions. For example, a guerrilla band operating in an area remote from civilian centers need not involve civilian damage. The Cuban insurgency against the Batista regime appears to have involved minimal civilian damage. The guerrillas fought primarily in remote mountainous country and restricted their fighting to hit-and-run attacks on military installations. It was only when the Cuban army had clearly failed to defeat the guerrillas that the latter marched on the cities, where they fought in a more or less conventional way. So it is certainly *possible* that guerrilla warfare could be fought with discrimination, providing the combatants can be separated from the noncombatants. This may be accomplished either by the insurgents removing themselves from civilian centers *or* by the counterinsurgents separating the "fish from the water," as was successfully accomplished in Malaya (and unsuccessfully in Vietnam).

The foregoing kinds of exception seem rare. The temptation to "short-cut" *jus in bello* is very great. But there is a moral and practical price to pay for this deviation, as the selection from Liddell-Hart makes clear (see Appendix).

We may conclude, then, that of the two forms of conflict which are said to present a special challenge to *bellum justum,* guerrilla warfare is the one likely to prevail in future. Nuclear warfare, whether counterforce or countervalue, is unacceptable for moral and prudential reasons. Nuclear weapons are essentially instruments of terror and may be ruled out under the principle of discrimination.

Guerrilla warfare does present certain problems for both insurgents and counterinsurgents. Ideally, guerrilla warfare ought to be activated only as a last resort in a situation where conventional fighting is not possible. Guerrilla war *can* be fought justly, but because of its potential problems (widening of the target and creating a conflict of wills) it is the least desirable form of warfare, though under some circumstances it may be the lesser of evils. Needless to say, terrorism ought to be eschewed in all forms of warfare and in this one particularly, given the clear potential for such evil. Counterinsurgency may also be conducted justly if two conditions are kept in mind: First, in view of the possibility of a blurred line between combatants and noncombatants, conventional forces and firepower ought to be employed in a counterinsurgency role as a last resort only. Special forces trained for anti-guerrilla warfare and augmented by the constabulary of the host country stand a better chance of being able to conduct this form of war justly.

Second, our concept of war as a crusade of limited duration must be changed. We must come to see counterinsurgency in the context of nation building, a process which may take a generation or more and, like the fight against crime, may never be entirely successful.

Chapter 4

Pacifism and Realpolitik

IT IS BEST to begin by trying to sort out some of the varieties of pacifism. It is obviously not enough to say that pacifists are people who oppose war or who are against the use of force. Nor will it do to characterize pacifism in terms of certain positive beliefs, such as an ultimate regard for the sanctity of human life. These are beliefs to which any moral agent would certainly subscribe. What makes pacifism philosophically interesting is not its principled belief that violence is evil but, as Jan Narveson puts it, the belief that "it is morally wrong to use force to resist, punish, or prevent violence. This further step makes pacifism a radical moral doctrine."[1]

Let us label this position "intrinsicalism" and contrast it with what I shall call "tactical" pacifism. Someone who believes that it is morally permissible to use force to resist or prevent violence might adopt the pacifist stance as a purely tactical matter. He might judge that pacifism is likely to be the best *means* of bringing about peace. This could happen in at least two ways. It might be thought that pacifism is the appropriate response because of peculiar historical circumstances. Thus, India in 1946 and the United States in the 1960s could be seen as places where nonviolent resistance would be an appropriate tactic. In both of those places the rule of law obtained to the degree that the penalties for such disobedience were relatively mild, and there was a chance that such tactics might succeed. However, the same person could well decide that pacifism was not obligatory in Nazi Germany or Stalinist Russia.

101

Someone might also adopt tactical pacifism based upon a judgment about the actual possibility of using force justly in the modern era. While admitting the theoretical possibility of justified force, it may be thought that as long as certain sorts of weapons are retained, or as long as terror is officially sanctioned, then a justified war simply cannot be fought.

Both of these versions of tactical pacifism are compatible with *bellum justum;* indeed, they are entailed by that doctrine. Neither makes an a priori commitment to the position that the use of force will always, under all conceivable circumstances, be wrong. The behavior of the tactical pacifist may be indistinguishable from that of the intrinsicalist on many occasions, but the former leaves open the question of whether force is justified in a given circumstance, and this marks an important moral difference. Thus, intrinsicalism is the only version of pacifism which can be described as a moral position opposed to *bellum justum.* In Narveson's words, "To hold the pacifist position as a genuine, full-blooded moral principle is to hold that nobody has a right to fight back when attacked, that fighting back is inherently evil, as such. It means we are all mistaken in supposing we have a right of self-protection."[2]

Narveson argues that what I have called intrinsicalism is a genuine moral position in virtue of its claim that the use of force in self-defense is in itself evil and that pacifism is incumbent on everyone, not just those who happen to believe that the use of force is evil. So intrinsicalism satisfies the Kantian test for calling a particular principle a moral imperative. Narveson's objection to pacifism is directed toward what he claims are logical inconsistencies in the principle itself. For the belief that the use of force is inherently evil must minimally entail that people have a right not to be the object of violent attacks. At least part of what must be meant by saying that a particular action is wrong is that people have a right not to have that sort of thing done to them; they have a right to take steps to prevent the abridgement of that right. This is an interesting line of argument because its effectiveness depends not upon an opposed set of moral principles but upon an analysis of what it means to possess a right in general. If the notion of "having a right" is to make any sort of sense, if it is not be be merely an expression, then to say that someone has a right must also be to say that he is justified in taking steps to prevent that right from being abridged. The "must" is a logical must:

To say that you have a right to X but no one has any justification whatever for preventing people from depriving you of it, is self-contradictory. If you claim a right to X, then to describe some action as an act of depriving you of X, is logically to imply that its absence is one of the things you have a right to.[3]

A pacifist might well reply that this logical point, while sound, is not a description of his position. What Narveson shows is that if a person has a right, he cannot also have a duty to be purely passive in the face of an attack upon that right. Of course, the pacifist will insist that his is not a doctrine of passivity or fatalism. As a moral agent, he is concerned with ethical imperatives, with guiding action. So the question becomes not whether a person does or does not have a duty to acquiesce in the removal of one of his rights but, rather, what level of force is appropriate in face of a violent attack. Narveson might well reply that the commitment *always* to refrain from violence is in effect a permission to abrogate his rights. For if an opponent knows in advance that the pacifist will only resist up to the level of actual fighting, then he will simply escalate his attacks beyond that point. This is precisely what happened when nonviolent resistance was tried briefly in Nazi-occupied Norway.

There is one way of attempting to get around this internal contradiction which intrinsicalism appears to carry with it. Instead of seeing pacifism as a "moral position" in the ordinary sense, perhaps we should understand it as a commitment to an ideal type. The pacifist will concentrate on developing into the kind of person for whom nonviolence is a permanent part of the soul, and by example he will encourage others to do the same. The pacifist would admit that the world does contain men who commit violent attacks upon others, but his concern will be to demonstrate by his own example that an alternative way of life is possible: men do not have to take life; they do not have to adopt the posture of the utilitarian bargainer. This kind of "saintliness" does, however, seem irresponsible. The unwillingness of the pacifist to dirty his hands is no doubt the source of the charge that he is more concerned about the state of his soul than with the preservation of life. The unwillingness to kill or injure may be part of the pacifist's very being, but what happens to his "respect for life" defense when his refusal to fight causes loss of lives which could have been saved? Critics of the argument that pacifism is part of a program to attain an ideal of selfhood respond with the charge of "moral egoism."

It [moral egoism] differs from ordinary egoism only in its allegedly spiritual quality. It is a thoroughgoing refusal to dirty one's own hands. . . . I suggest that those whose concerns are thus limited are warped, self-righteous and ultimately self-serving. The pacifist "saint" who stands by while others are being murdered or brutalized . . . how does he differ from a moral idiot, except in point of pretentiousness?[4]

The alternative to intrinsicalism is tactical pacifism. As was suggested earlier, the argument that passive resistance will bring about desirable ethical consequences is a factual claim. The belief that nonviolent resistance will be effective in face of aggression may be challenged only in terms of factual claims or predictions to the contrary, not on first principles. The main line of argument here is based upon an appeal to the essential goodness of human nature. On this view war is fundamentally a corruption of man's nature, and it is implausible to think a lasting peace could be produced by resort to arms. No matter what the noble intentions of the warmakers, the practical effect of war is the denigration of man. No matter what the historical period, men will always be able to find "good reasons" for fighting. Pacifism will never find the "right" time to come into being. We must simply say: From henceforth we will try a new tactic to oppose violence. Defense against aggression will accordingly exploit only those qualities which will preserve human integrity. As Gordon Zahn puts it:

Therefore, our means of defense must be so organized and our policies so developed that they find their effectiveness in the identification and exploitation of the essentially human qualities and capacities in ourselves and the potential enemy and not in the continued effort to destroy the greatest possible number of "them" at the least possible cost to "cost."[5]

Nonviolence, on this view, is openly admitted to entail the exercise of force. The crucial difference between violent and nonviolent resistance lies in the means employed to bring about peace. While *bellum justum* insists that a necessary limitation on war is that it remain a contest of strength, pacifism makes war a contest of will. The pacifist will meet aggression not with the weapons of war but with the power of the will and the spirit. Two historical examples of this are Gandhi's "soul force" and the "power of love." Moreover, the aggressor must be met not merely by individuals who are committed to nonviolence but by an organized pacifist "army" well trained in the strategy and tactics of nonviolence.

The putative practicality of pacifism as a means resides in the doctrine of a common human nature.

The nonviolence alternative is keyed to a universalistic identity with and concern for the humanity inherent in all men, including the potential aggressor. And this, in turn, is expected at some point to trigger a reciprocal response in the opposing party; to fan, so to speak, the spark of human decency which, no matter how low it may burn in individual men for a time, cannot be extinguished completely or forever.[6]

It is a trait of "idealistic" theories generally that they are willing to mortgage the present to the future. In line with this, the pacifist is willing to sacrifice lives to aggression as a means of breaking the circle of recurring warfare. He has to believe that ultimately his teaching methods will work. Since people's lives are being put on the line for this belief, it might be expected that pacifists would be prepared to say at what point nonviolent resistance would have to be abandoned. That is, how much killing would have to take place to cause the pacifist to give up his belief in a common human nature responsive at some point in history to pacifist methods? In fact, pacifists tend to be unclear on this point. In discussing the consequences of noncooperation with an aggressor nation, Gordon Zahn admits that the casualties which pacifists would suffer initially may be expected to be considerable. But there must, he thinks, be some limit to aggressiveness.

At some point the totalitarian automaton will have to act as a man; and this will be, for him, the breaking point. Only so many trains will run over so many bodies before the trains stop running altogether; only so many hostages will be executed before the executioners refuse to shed any more innocent blood. Perhaps it is starry-eyed idealism to speak of such limits; but to deny that they exist and that they must ultimately be reached would be a denial of the very dignity and humanity of man, the recognition of which we claim as the hallmark of our way of life and the justification of its defense.[7]

In short, *unless* men can be persuaded to be ultimately peaceful there is no real point in regarding others as having any moral status at all. Civilized life as we know it is a sham unless the propensity to violence can be shown to be an accidental, in principle expungeable, feature of human culture. This is an extraordinary view, bordering on fanaticism, for it really demands a temporal appearance of human perfection.

Both the pacifist and the adherent of *bellum justum* are in agreement that direct attacks upon other people are morally wrong, but the pacifist will not accept the distinction between intentional and unintentional killing in war. That is, the pacifist will reject as meaningless any attempt to escape culpability for murder by distinguishing between intention and foreknowledge — anyone taking up arms in a war has perfectly clear foreknowledge that his actions will result in the death of many people. Now, if the pacifist does make this argument, then surely he is open to his own criticism. For in a war between pacifists and ruthless aggressors, such as the Nazis or the Soviets, the pacifists would also have perfectly clear foreknowledge that *their* refusal to bear arms would result in the deaths of a great many people who could have been saved if they had been prepared to use force to save them. The difference seems to be that the pacifist will not "dirty his hands" by countering force with force.

There is another sense in which pacifism might be said to have undesirable consequences. Zahn speaks of "breaking" the totalitarian automaton. This is symptomatic of the tendency of pacifism to convert war from a trial of strength to a trial of will. Pacifism, that is, has a tendency to make conflict total by targeting the will of the adversary. If this works, then the aggressor will be converted, and all will be well. But a failure to convert him may well make his response more severe than if he had been opposed by force to arms. This is in contrast with a trial of strength in which the use of force may be the means of settling a dispute without requiring a fundamental alteration of the values of the combatants. In other words, if the parties to a conflict can be persuaded to accept the decision of arms, they may be allowed to come away with their beliefs and value systems substantially intact. The losing side must accept the verdict of the conqueror; but if they have fought as bravely and efficiently as could be expected, then their view of themselves may continue relatively unchanged. It is in this sense that resort to arms may be a way of "encapsulating" a conflict. What the pacifist proposes is to make every conflict which cannot be settled by rational persuasion an occasion for attempted conversion. The aggressor must either give in or kill the pacifists. It is these stark alternatives which lead to the pacifist conception of conflict as "total."

In spite of these and similar criticisms, it remains the case that a great many people who are not pacifists themselves look with favor upon that position. There is the wistful suggestion in many of these accolades that we all really *ought* to be pacifists but that weakness of will, selfishness, or even uncontrollable temper intervenes to prevent that. "I could not restrain myself from fighting back if someone attacked me, but I admire those who are so committed to their principles that they would die before using violence" is the sort of sentiment which one frequently hears in this regard. How are we to explain the respect which pacifism evokes in people who are themselves prepared to use violence? Part of the answer is undoubtedly that very few people who think that resorting to force is sometimes justified believe force to be anything but a necessary evil. If force *is* evil, then perhaps the logical thing is to eschew it altogether. The pacifist position appears simple, clear-cut, and, above all, clean. Not having carefully thought out a position on the justified use of force, and noting the frequent misuses of force throughout history, the ordinary man is likely to conclude that the pacifist is right, even if most people are not sufficiently principled to imitate him. As Anscombe has pointed out, it is in this sense that the influence of pacifism is far greater than the number of its adherents would suggest:

Now pacifism teaches people to make no distinction between the shedding of innocent blood and the shedding of any human blood. And in this way pacifism has corrupted enormous numbers of people who will not act according to its tenets. They become convinced that a number of things are wicked which are not; hence, seeing no way of avoiding "wickedness," they set no limits to it. How endlessly pacifists argue that all war must be *à outrance*. That those who wage war must go as far as technological advance permits in the destruction of the enemy's people.[8]

These remarks once again reflect a curious similarity be-

tween pacifism and various forms of realpolitik. The pacifist can see no difference between wars which are fought
in self-defense and wars of brutal and blatant conquest.
The practical effect of this is that in an actual war he is
unprepared to offer any suggestion on how the conflict
might be limited. Anscombe's point is just that insofar as
pacifism is regarded as an ideal for the mass of men, it is
an ideal short of which they will inevitably fall. But the
damage will have been done. Having dirtied their hands
by resorting to evil means, there is no reason not to go all
the way and fight war à outrance as a means of securing
victory. If the use of force is evil, why limit ourselves
once we have chosen to fight? The evil is done by the first
act of violence; to embark upon war is to place oneself
outside the moral sphere, so what is to be gained by at-
tending to moral niceties while killing the enemy? If we
are to sin, let us sin well and truly.

In concluding this discussion, it is worthwhile to raise briefly
the question of the political relevance of pacifism. Most
pacifist writers agree that if pacifism is to be ultimately
successful it must advance beyond the level of individual
commitment. While pacifism will always be a personal decision to refrain from violence, its effectiveness as a political force will depend upon converting pacifism into a mass
movement. A program as rigid and uncompromising as is
found in any manual of military training will govern the
organization and conduct of the new army of nonviolent
resisters:

The ordinary man, whether he be the friendly young clerk at
the supermarket or the teacher called from his classroom, has
to be "made over," has to be taught to use and understand the
weapons of modern war and, most crucial of all, must be con-
ditioned to a level of virtually automatic and certainly unques-
tioning acceptance of the fact that he is expected to kill other
human beings. . . . It is not much different for nonviolence.[9]

The nonviolent soldier will have to be trained always to
respond to an attack upon himself and others with passive

resistance. It is important to understand that for the great majority of pacifists no particular political ideology is being advanced. Typically the pacifist is concerned not with policy options in the normal sense but with changing our fundamental conception of man as a creature whose "behavior is finally controlled through promises of physically satisfying rewards and threats of violently induced pain."[10]

Serious doubts may be raised about how such a program is to be developed within the present nation-state system. The proposal to instruct and train the youth of the nation in the theory and practice of pacifism presupposes that they will sit still for such indoctrination. The concept of conscription or, indeed, any sort of coercion at all seems alien to pacifist ideals and methods. The difficulty in organizing a pacifist army is compounded by pacifism's tendency to undermine the traditional concept of political obligation. It is normally supposed that there is a strong presumption in favor of obeying the commands of one's lawful sovereign. However, according to pacifists, this doctrine has been one of the major causes of war: "Somehow, if this pattern is ever to be broken, each individual must be convinced that he has the right and the competence to judge what is asked of him on the basis of the information available to him and that he can have some impact on the course of events, even if he must stand alone."[11] If the individual does have this right, then it is unlikely that very large numbers of people will opt for pacifism. The principle that individual conscience transcends political loyalty must certainly complicate any pacifist attempt to become the legitimate authority.

Pacifism appears to have had its greatest political effect in the area of nuclear disarmament. The Campaign for Nuclear Disarmament began in Britain in the 1950s and was able to enlist a remarkable degree of popular support before its demise in the 1960s. It is, however, unclear to what extent agitation to "Ban the Bomb" sprang from pure pacifist principles. Massive retaliation is unsatisfactory not only for pacifists but also for adherents of the political theory of war and of *bellum justum*. Indeed, one might very well argue that the evenhandedness of the pacifist militates against his being taken seriously, for he will oppose on principle all wars and all weapons systems, thus making impossible any kind of dispassionate assessment of this *particular* war or weapons system.

We may conclude, then, that pacifism of both forms is unsatisfactory. Intrinsicalism cannot make the claim that it is always wrong to use force compatible with the right not to have violence done to oneself. Tactical pacifism may be morally required under some limited circumstances. If civil disobedience is ever justified in a democratic setting, then there are good reasons for thinking that it ought to be nonviolent. But there are no good reasons for thinking that nonviolent resistance will always have ethically good consequences, particularly when it entails a temporal appearance of human perfection.

This section has been very difficult for me to write. In discussing these issues with pacifists over the past ten years or so, I have been much impressed with their moral concern and sincerity. I must reluctantly conclude, though, that pacifism is at its worst morally in error and at its best just plain muddled.

If we reject the standpoint of general pacifism, we are faced with the difficult problem of establishing criteria for selective refusal to be conscripted. It will be useful to begin by asking whether in a free society citizens have a standing or prima facie obligation to defend the state by force of arms. The *legal* institution of conscription presupposes that every citizen has such a duty, which can be overridden only by a more pressing obligation or by some attribute the citizen possesses which will make him more useful to the state as a noncombatant. There may also be the possibility of deferring service for socially useful ends.

Historically conscription was preceded by the press gang, whose function was to fill the ranks with soldiers who would be required to serve for anything up to twenty years. Impressment was a practice both arbitrary and un-expected, and those unlucky enough to get in the way of the press gang normally had no legal recourse. The practice was irregular, being used to supplement normal recruiting methods. On the whole those impressed were the lowest elements in the social scale. For this reason senior officers did not disapprove of this means of induction. As usual, they preferred rankers from the bottom of the barrel, since such men were tough, easily led, and lacking in social influence and political power.

The modern concept of conscription began with the French Revolution. The idea that citizens should have an equal share in the burdens as well as the benefits of the state made it seem quite natural that individuals would want to do their part in the defense of the state. Thus the draft was not perceived as a device for dragooning unwilling conscripts into the army but as a system for providing, in a constant and controlled manner, the opportunity for citizens to fulfil their moral obligation to participate in the defense of the state. The duty to serve in the armed forces was understood to be an instance of political obligation in general.[12]

Most modern critics of the draft who are not out-and-out pacifists argue that conscription in a democratic society involves a serious abridgement of the liberties of the citizen. The legal duty to serve in the forces is simply not on a par with other legal obligations, such as tax paying or having a valid driver's license. To remove a person from his normal life and place him under military law must always be regarded as an imposition unless it can be shown that there is an overriding necessity of state which requires it. So drastic is conscription's interference with liberty that only a threat to liberty itself can possibly justify it. As John Rawls puts it:

Conscription is permissible only if it is demanded for the defense of liberty itself, including here not only the liberties of the citizens of the society in question, but also those of persons in other societies as well. Therefore, if a conscript army is less likely to be an instrument of unjustified foreign adventures, it may be justified on this basis alone despite the fact that conscription infringes upon the equal liberties of citizens.[13]

Thus on Rawls's view an all-volunteer professional army might constitute a standing threat to liberty, in the sense that it could at any time be used in pursuit of unjust policies. On the somewhat dubious assumption that conscript armies make it more difficult to carry on unjust wars, we may conclude that conscription is justified even where there is no immediate threat to liberty such as a foreign invasion.

It might be argued that once a person accepts the legitimacy of conscription he must assent to induction even if the army is engaged in a war which he regards as unjust. This is so because the mere fact of conscription does not mean that he has been asked to do anything which could be considered immoral. To be conscripted cannot be supposed to be immoral as such. Of course, if someone regards it as highly probable that he will be sent to fight in a war of which he morally disapproves, then he may decide that refusal to obey orders will become progressively more difficult for him as he approaches the combat situation. Thus he may opt to refuse induction altogether. There is certainly some merit to this position, if for no other reason than that once in the army he may find himself coerced in various ways into doing things which he finds unacceptable on moral grounds. The fact that coercion will exculpate him does not cancel the fact that the deed was done and that he was part of it.

The main pitfall that selective conscientious objection must avoid is slipping into a generalized pacifism war by war. To prevent this from happening we must undertake the hard intellectual effort involved in determining if a specific war involves injustice sufficient to oppose it. Moreover, we must build defenses and safeguards into existing military and civil law so that the individual soldier or draftee will not have to bear the full burden of proof himself.

Another major problem in trying to make selective objection work will be to devise a test for conscientiousness. We must, that is, find some way of distinguishing between those who object to a particular war on moral grounds and those who are using their objection to advance a political ideology. An absolute pacifist assures us of his sincerity by opting out of all wars. He may indeed have political objections to a particular war, but these are overridden by his commitment to nonviolence. He offers no particular threat to the state, since he would reject war no matter what the political circumstances. This is a crucial point, because before any government can allow men to select the wars in which they will participate, it would have to be assured that there is some way of distinguishing political partisanship from moral conviction:

We must face the fact, in other words, that no political society can allow exemption for purely political objection to its uses of military force. . . . Without the manifold intellectual work that is needed to wrestle successfully with this distinction, the proposal of selective objection will remain an ideological protest— or else one that is based on the optimistic faith of philosophical anarchism that out of the self-determining freedom of individual consciences political community can be composed and its energies directed effectively one way rather than another in the course of history.[14]

Is it conceivable that governments might grant selective objection the same legal status as it gives to pacifism? The answer, I fear, is no. And that tells us something important about pacifism. Governments are prepared to tolerate pacifism, because it poses no threat either to their political policies or to the manner in which wars are conducted. The pacifist objects equally to all wars waged by all governments. In this sense he opts out of the game altogether. By contrast, the selective objector will be forced to analyze both the policy decisions of the government as well as the conduct of the armed forces. He will be publicly carrying out an officially sanctioned comparison between mutually agreed just-war criteria and the actual performance of the government. That is a lot to expect of governments as we know them, but there is still more. What would be the implication of a state *granting* an exemption on selective grounds? Fundamentally, the state would be agreeing with the claim that its war policies may be reasonably interpreted as unjust. The belief that *all* war is wrong is a proposition which states might agree is debatable among rational men, and, therefore, claims to exemption on this basis may be allowed. It is a very different matter, however, to grant exemption for a particular war, for here we are faced not with two philosophical theories about violence but with a factual dispute. Selective objection presupposes that both the government and the claimant agree upon the criteria for undertaking a justified war and the rules for conducting it. The claimant would have to show, in order to qualify for an exemption, that his government is engaged in acts of war which a person might reasonably characterize as immoral. As such an admission is inseparable from policy questions, it is inconceivable that any government would be willing (or politically able) to wage war while publicly agreeing that there is sufficient reason to doubt the morality of that war to grant exemptions from it. This is not to say that individuals should not refuse to fight in wars which they believe are immoral but to acknowledge that governments cannot be expected to institutionalize such a practice. The evenhandedness of the pacifist who objects to all wars does not threaten the particular policies of any state. In condemning them all equally, pacifism exempts itself from political reality:

What is needed, then, is not a general pacifism but a discriminating conscientious refusal to engage in war in certain circumstances. States have not been loath to recognize pacifism and to grant it a special status. The refusal to take part in all war under any conditions is an unworldly view bound to remain a sectarian doctrine. It no more challenges the state's authority than the celibacy of priests challenges the sanctity of marriage. By exempting pacifists from its prescriptions the state may even seem to display a certain magnanimity. But conscientious refusal based upon the principles of justice as they apply to particular conflicts is another matter. For such refusal is an affront to the government's pretensions, and when it becomes widespread, the continuation of an unjust war may prove impossible.[15]

Pacifism and realpolitik are in agreement on the question of the relation of morality to statecraft, particularly in the area of war: both presuppose an unbridgeable gap between the two. As we have seen, the pacifist solution to the supposed disjunction is effectively to abandon politics. Of course, he continues to live in political society but fails to realize, or perhaps to admit, that the stability of his society is ultimately dependent upon the willingness to use force. The realist, on the other hand, immerses himself in politics by fully uniting his intentions with state necessity as he perceives it. Thus, while their solutions to the disjunction differ radically, their diagnosis of the problem, namely, that statecraft is evil, is the same, a verdict sometimes rendered by the pacifist in idioms of saintly denunciation and by the realist in the vocabulary of a resigned stoicism.

The doctrine of realpolitik (sometimes called the political theory of war), to which we may now turn, is not new. Its first exponent was no doubt Thrasymachus and its most notorious, Machiavelli. I shall, however, turn to the father figure of modern realpolitik, especially as that doctrine bears upon the problem of war: Karl von Clausewitz.

Clausewitz was a soldier who had fought in the wars against Napoleon, serving with particular prominence in the Moscow campaigns of 1812 and 1813. He was impressed with the changes which Bonaparte had brought to warfare, in particular the concentration of force leading to a crushing blow against the enemy. The aggressive characteristic of Napoleon's armies was made possible by the ideological climate created by the French Revolution. For the first time in modern history, soldiers were imbued with a sense of mission—they were saving the revolution and France. War for them was no longer a matter between princes. War was now the people's business. Against such motivation the armies of the ancien régime simply melted away. Their mercenary base, their tactics of "demonstration," and their inability to undertake pursuit made them completely vulnerable to the new armies of Napoleon. To Clausewitz, the destruction of the old-style "cabinet" wars of the eighteenth century, with their rigorous codes of behavior, appeared to signal a wholly new step in the evolution of warfare, a step which required analysis and explanation. It was to this task that Clausewitz was to devote his remaining days.

From 1818 to 1830 he was director of the Military Academy at Berlin, where he formulated his famous philosophy of war. He died in the cholera epidemic which swept Berlin in 1831, an epidemic which also killed Hegel. *On War* was published by his wife in 1832.

Clausewitz was a student of Kant, and he considered himself a Kantian. It is important to understand this fact, because Clausewitz adopts what he conceives to be the Kantian methodology in his analysis of war. This consists of considering a concept in its pure or "absolute" state, shorn of any empirical content, and then trying to understand its relation to the world. Just as Kant isolated and explicated the pure categories of the understanding before delineating their empirical content in his epistemology, so Clausewitz seeks first to understand the concept of war as it is in itself before going on to detail the application of the idea to reality. A failure to grasp this methodological device resulted, as we shall see, in widespread misunderstanding of Clausewitz, particularly by historians and military men. They tended to concentrate on the absolute concept of war and neglect what Clausewitz had to say about real war. As Liddell-Hart puts it:

His theory of war was expounded in a way too abstract and involved for ordinary soldier-minds, essentially concrete, to follow
the course of his argument—which often turned back from the
direction in which it was leading. Impressed yet befogged, they
grasped at his vivid leading phrases, seeing only their surface
meaning, and missing the deeper currents of his thought. [16]

Clausewitz begins by defining war as an instantaneous
blow without duration. This is, of course, a definition of
absolute war—of what war would be like were it completely ideal. This means that there are no factors intrinsic
to the idea of war which might restrain its headlong rush
toward absolute violence. War, then, is an act of violence
intended to compel an opponent to fulfil our will. The concept of such an act has its own internal logic—a kind of
self-development which ideally would necessarily lead to
an explosion of absolute violence. It follows that the rules
of war are external to war as such: "Self-imposed restrictions, almost imperceptible and hardly worth mentioning,
termed usages of International Law, accompany it without
essentially impairing its power.[17]

Clausewitz labels as "philanthropy" any attempt to restrain violence:

Now philanthropists may easily imagine there is a skillful method
of disarming and overcoming an enemy without causing great
bloodshed, and that this is the proper tendency of the Art of
War. However plausible this may appear, still it is an error
which must be extirpated; for in such dangerous things as War,
the errors which proceed from a spirit of benevolence are the
worst. This is the way the matter must be viewed, and it is to
no purpose, it is even against one's own interest, to turn away
from the consideration of the real nature of the affair because
the horror of its elements excites repugnance.

If the Wars of civilized peoples are less cruel and destructive
than those of savages, the difference arises from the social condition of States in themselves and in their relations to each other.
Out of this social condition and its relations War arises, and by it
War is subjected to conditions, is controlled and modified. But
these things do not belong to War itself; they are only given con-

ditions; and to introduce into the philosophy of War itself a principle of moderation would be an absurdity.[18]

Two passions lie at the heart of war: instinctive hostility and hostile intention. Clausewitz argues that the apparent "civilizing" of war in the eighteenth century by making it more and more an act of intelligence is a dangerous illusion, an illusion exploded in the transition from cabinet wars to the wars of nations in 1812. The restraints on war current in the wars prior to Bonaparte only mask the underlying passionate hatred of one nation for another. Philosophy of war was beginning to drift in the direction of seeing combat as a pure act of the intelligence, a board game using real people, until Bonaparte shattered that conception forever: "The invention of gunpowder, the constant progress of improvements in the construction of firearms, are sufficient proofs that the tendency do destroy the adversary which lies at the bottom of the conception of War is in no way changed or modified through the progress of civilization.[19]

For Clausewitz war is an act of violence pushed to its utmost bounds, and it comprises the sum of available means plus the strength of the will. As war is always the clash of two animate bodies (armies), violence will necessarily escalate toward the absolute limit until one or the other is defeated. The logic of violence and the interplay of the passions is such that once war is embarked upon, there is nothing in principle which constrains it from escalating to the level of absolute war: an instantaneous blow without duration. The notion of prohibitions and restraints in war is only a transitory cultural phenomenon, "hardly worth mentioning."

This conception of war as a violent clash necessarily leading toward the extreme, motivated by hatred and carried out through a mobilization of all available means, is prophetic of the adherence to his own gospel in World Wars I and II. Liddell-Hart:

For it was the ideal and not the practical aspect of his teaching on war which survived. He contributed to the distortion by arguing that it was only to avoid the risks of battle that "any other means are taken." And he fixed the distortion in the minds of his pupils by hammering on the abstract ideal.

Not one reader in a hundred was likely to follow the subtlety of his logic or to preserve a true balance amid such philosophical jugglery. But everyone could catch such ringing phrases as:

"We have only one means in War—the battle."

"The bloody solution of the crisis, the effort for the destruction of the enemy's forces, is the first-born son of war."

"Let us not hear of generals who conquer without bloodshed."

By the reiteration of such phrases, Clausewitz blurred the outlines of his philosophy, already indistinct, and made it into a mere marching refrain—a Prussian *Marseillaise* which inflamed the blood and intoxicated the mind. In transfusion it became a doctrine fit to form corporals, not generals.[20]

The interpretation of Clausewitz which thus passed into history is one which sees war as the determining factor in policy and not the other way around. If war has its own inner logic, if it necessarily escalates toward absolute force, then the decision to embark upon war is the signal that statecraft has failed. The transition from peace to war is a move from rationality and order to passion and the "fog of battle." Under these circumstances *bellum justum* will have to be understood as a kind of category mistake—a pathetic attempt to apply moral reasoning in a situation which is precisely its antithesis. Now one of the most interesting points about this concept of war is that it is identical with the pacifist's view. Both see war as essentially unconnected with statecraft and as arising not out of and controlled by any concrete policy. We have already noted Anscombe's remark, "How endlessly pacifists argue that all wars must be fought *à outrance*." The pacifist solution is to abandon statecraft because it is unable to prevent war, while those who have fastened upon the ideal aspect of Clausewitz's theories have chosen to embrace war in its "purity." This latter position led, in the late nineteenth and early twentieth centuries, to an enormous amount of advocacy of war as having therapeutic value. Writers such as Bernhardi, Ludendorf, Junger, and numerous Frenchmen under the spell of Bergson wrote of the glories of war and of the necessity of war as a means of "cleansing" the human spirit. Thus was established in the minds of men a belief that war must necessarily be absolute and that the only responses possible are pacifism or realpolitik.

These stark alternatives are possible only because, as Liddell-Hart has noted, readers of Clausewitz fastened upon what he had to say about war as an "ideal" concept. The application of the pure concept of war to reality was missed in the heady discussion of violence and bloodshed. In fact, the Clausewitzian philosophy of war turns out to be, in my opinion, not very different from *bellum justum* when fully set out and understood. Let us turn to a brief examination of the "other side" of Clausewitz.

He begins with the question: Given the absolute concept of war, can it ever be realized empirically? It *could* be if three conditions were realized: (1) if war arises spontaneously, without any connection with previous political conditions; (2) "if it is limited to a single solution or to several simultaneous solutions"; (3) if war itself contains its own solution without any consideration of the political *consequences* of fighting.

It was the opinion of Clausewitz that none of these conditions could ever possibly exist. In the first place, war is never an isolated act. The knowledge which each side has of the other prevents war from starting instantly or moving to an extreme automatically. These "deficiencies," as Clausewitz calls them, become a modifying principle. Secondly, war is *not* an instantaneous blow without duration. In reality, all forces are not brought forward at once:

Now it is possible to bring all the movable military forces of a country into operation at once, but not all fortresses, rivers, mountains, people, etc.—in short, not the whole country, unless it is so small that it can be embraced by the first act of war. Further, the cooperation of the allies does not depend upon the Will of the belligerents; and from the nature of the political relations of states to each other, this cooperation is frequently not afforded until the War has commenced, or it may be increased to restore the balance of power.[21]

Clausewitz concludes that a complete concentration of all available means in a moment of time is an ideal that could never be realized: "Finally, War does not carry with it an absolute solution: The conquered State often sees in it only a passing evil, which may be repaired in after times by means of political combinations. How much this must modify the degree of tension, and the vigour of the efforts made, is evident in itself."[22]

These political and other modifications are characterized by Clausewitz as "friction." This is an illuminating term, because it reveals that he is thinking of the escalation of war, on the ideal level, as essentially mechanistic. Moreover, it is clear that Clausewitz regards these modifications as unfortunate. Like the inventor of the perpetual-motion machine, he thinks of "friction" as the archenemy. In short, Clausewitz was fascinated by and enjoyed war as an intense human experience. The experience would be at its most intense if war could actually move to an absolute. Unfortunately, the empirical application of the ideal concept results in a certain amount of "drag," always causing actual wars to fall short of the ideal. Thus, the political object which initiated the war is allowed to reassert itself.

The reappearance of the political object means that war is now subject to intelligent control and that the application of force must be directed to particular ends rather than toward maximization of force as such. As Clausewitz emphasizes continually, however, war is no mere pastime, no mere desire for venturing and winning, no work of a free enthusiasm: it is a serious means for a serious object:

The War of a community—of whole Nations, and particularly of civilized Nations—always starts from a political condition, and is called forth by a political motive. It is, therefore, a political act. Now if it was a perfect, unrestrained, and absolute expression of force, as we had to deduce from its mere conception, then the moment it is called forth by policy, it would step into the place of policy, and as something quite independent of it would set it aside, and only follow its own laws, just as a mine at the moment of explosion cannot be guided into any other direction than that which has been given to it by preparatory arrangements. But it is not so, and the idea is radically false: War in the real world is not an extreme thing which expends itself at one single discharge. Now, if we reflect that War has its root in a political object, then naturally this original motive which called it into existance should also continue the first and highest consideration in its conduct. Still the political object is no despotic lawgiver on that account; it must accomodate itself to the nature of the means, and though changes in these means may involve modification in the political objective, the latter *always* retains a prior right to consideration. Policy, therefore, is interwoven with the whole action of War and must exercise a continuous influence upon it, as far as the nature of the forces liberated by it will permit.[23]

War is, therefore, not only a political act but also an instrument of policy and a continuation of policy, "a carrying out of the same by other means." This view of the nature of war is quite clearly directly opposite to that espoused by many of Clausewitz's "disciples." War is not a "thing in itself"; it does not represent the failure of statecraft but is itself merely one among many *means* of effecting state interest. War and peace are inextricably intertwined; they are different phases of the same thing: the continuing dialectic of power between states. The belief that war must always be fought à outrance is a mistaken belief based upon the misconception that when war is undertaken, a transition is made from rationality to irrationality; that war and peace are virtually different ontological realms:

Is not War merely another kind of writing and language for political thoughts? It has certainly a grammar of its own, but its logic is not peculiar to itself. This kind of idea would be indispensable even if War was perfect War, the perfectly unbridled element of hostility, for all the circumstances on which it rests, and which determined its leading features, are they not of a political nature, and are they not so intimately connected with the whole political intercourse that it is impossible to separate them? But this view is doubly indispensable if we reflect that real War is no such consistent effort tending to an extreme, as it should be according to the abstract idea, but a half-and-half thing, a contradiction in itself.[24]

Now if Clausewitz is correct in arguing that the political object is paramount in war, then his "disciples" (and pacifists) are wrong in supposing that war must always be fought à outrance. As I have argued throughout this work, a political program which has any claim to rationality will not be effected by its proponents' use of means which are themselves likely to counter the policy. Historically this realization has led to the formulation of rules of war and of provisions for the discriminate and proportionate application of force. I need not repeat these arguments here. It is enough to say that an immoral political policy will almost certainly be inept, and the attempt to implement any political program by immoral means will ultimately be counterproductive. There is no inconsistency between *bellum justum* and realpolitik rightly conceived; and if anyone conceived it rightly, it was surely Clausewitz. Clausewitz is interesting because he is forced to admit the restraining hand of policy (and indirectly of *bellum justum*) against his will. He, like many professional soldiers, would so obviously prefer it if the means alone determined policy: if it *can* be done, it *ought* to be done. Yet he was perceptive enough to see the total unreality of such a position.

As we noted earlier, the followers of Clausewitz actually contributed to the divorce of war from statecraft by abstracting passages from his writings which emphasized war as an ideal concept.

At the very beginning of my discussion of *bellum justum* I quoted Robert Tucker's remark that defenders of the rules of war are attempting to "square the circle" in admitting that states are judges in their own cases and yet are limited in the means which they may take in seeing to their interests. Tucker's "square circle" is Clausewitz's "half-and-half thing, a contradiction in itself." Yet, unlike Tucker, Clausewitz realizes that while states may indeed be the final judge of what are their interests, states cannot be said to have any interests which can only be satisfied by resort to *any* means whatever. To put it shortly, a "policy" entails a political society, a moral community guided by reason and prudence. If war is an act and an instrument of policy, then it will be restrained at least minimally by those underlying principles. Thus, a realpolitik which understands war simply in terms of means is ultimately "unrealistic."

As Bernard Brodie has succinctly put the matter in a discussion of morality and state interest:

While morality by its very nature must finally be justified entirely on its own terms, it is not amiss to remind ourselves that especially in this world of abundant and rapid communications, any of our policies abroad that are either conspicuously immoral to begin with or likely to lapse into behavior that can easily be so labelled, whether justly or not so justly, is likely to prove quite inexpedient and ultimately self-defeating.[25]

Yet there is, it seems to me, a much more interesting and profound relationship between Clausewitz and *bellum justum* than simply that of compatibility. For Augustine, war is an inevitable product of human sinfulness. To limit violence, God has instituted the political state within which men can find protection and some measure of divine justice, which is to be distributed by the Christian prince under the direct guidance of God. Thus, one purpose of the state is to see that wars are limited. The provisions of *bellum justum* are directed toward this end. Clausewitz's teaching can be seen as a continuation of the claim that war must be no more than an instrument of politics, a teaching which will tend to guarantee that violence is limited. But Clausewitz may also be understood as sounding a warning: in the modern (post-Napoleonic) era we are in grave danger of seeing war as having a life entirely of its own. This, I think, is the essential meaning of Clausewitz. War *does* have a life of its own, but only on the purely ideal level. Politicians will make a terrible error if they allow soldiers to forget this, for the latter, involved as they are with the prosecution of the war, will necessarily perceive all matters in military terms. In the cabinet wars of the eighteenth century this did not matter very much, for political and military considerations were extremely closely coordinated. With the coming of Bonaparte, however, matters took a dramatic turn. Napoleonic tactics tend to detach war from its political moorings — concentration of overwhelming force and fire-power, the complete destruction of the enemy, vigorous pursuit, conscription, the mobilization of all national resources, and the pursuit of war for the sake of glory — all of which tend to carry violence beyond the control of politics. It will never, of course, actually attain a total divorce from statecraft (a logical impossibility for Clausewitz), but there is now the possibility of a very large wedge being driven between war and politics. Historical proof of this possibility can be seen in the career of Bonaparte after 1805. Before that date his war plans had made a certain amount of sense in terms of a pan-European union dominated by France. The failure of this idea did not, however, have the effect of dissuading Bonaparte from further fighting. After 1805 he continued to fight simply for the sake of victory.

The introduction by Bonaparte of the concept of victory (which means the total destruction of the enemy on the battlefield) is of the first importance. It was the main lesson which the "soldier-disciples" of Clausewitz learned from the master, and from reading him in conjunction with a study of the Napoleonic wars. The indications are clear, though, that Clausewitz regarded this notion as potentially disastrous. For in the wholehearted and obsessive pursuit of overwhelming victory at all costs, war becomes progressively detached from the guiding hand of policy; its violence and fury simply overshadow the authority of the civil order. This possibility was obscured by the period of relative peace between 1815 and 1914 (the so-called Pax Britanica) and by the Franco-Prussian War of 1870, whose brevity appeared to confirm the efficiency and "humanity" of the pursuit of total victory: the war was short and the casualties not severely high. It was not until World War I that the futility of conceiving of war as the pursuit of total victory on the battlefield became evident — at least to some.

World War I will stand as an everlasting monument to the madness of divorcing war from statecraft (and from *jus ad bellum*). The war was fought for reasons which, when not totally obscure, were meaningless; and it continued with frightful loss of life long after anyone could recall the putative "reason why." Military figures such as Douglas Haig and Ludendorff, in their all-consuming desire to defeat the other side no matter what the cost in human life and suffering, were led, strategically, to conduct the war with little or no concern for political aims and, tactically, to squander the lives of their men in futile frontal assaults. The political leaders of Europe stood for the most part mute. When they did speak up they were usually right and their military advisors wrong, as when Lloyd George instituted the convoy system over the protests of the navy, an action which prevented Britain from being starved out.

The conclusion of World War I did not, however, bring the extinction of the Napoleonic concept of victory. In World War II it returned in the guise of "unconditional surrender" and in the willingness to use massively destructive firepower against civilian populations. And the concept is still with us, bedeviling us through Korea and Vietnam. The last two wars represented efforts to fight for limited objectives with limited means. Interestingly, such efforts meant reviving certain medieval terms associated with *bellum justum*, such as *sanctuary* (the word used to describe our refusal to bomb enemy bases in Manchuria or even the Chinese end of the bridges across the Yalu). One should also note the persistent refusal to use nuclear weapons in both Korea and Vietnam, even though there was continuous pressure from the military to do so. The following is an excerpt from a meeting of the National Security Council with President Kennedy in 1962. General Lyman L. Lemnitzer, chairman of the Joint Chiefs of Staff,

outlined the process by which each American action [in Vietnam] would provoke a Chinese counteraction, provoking in turn an even more drastic American response. He concluded: "If we are given the right to use nuclear weapons we can guarantee victory." The President sat glumly rubbing his upper molar saying nothing. After a moment someone said, "Mr. President, perhaps you would have the General explain to us what he means by victory." Kennedy grunted and dismissed the meeting. Later he said, "Since he couldn't think of any further escalation, he would *have* to promise us victory."[26]

We also have from Korea the immortal words of General Douglas MacArthur: "There is no substitute for victory." MacArthur was denied permission to, among other things, use Formosan troops to invade the Chinese mainland, bomb Manchuria with nuclear weapons, and spread a belt of radioactive cobalt, several miles wide, across the Korean peninsula as a means of "trapping" Chinese forces.

The saga of MacArthur's dismissal by President Truman is interesting because it reveals the way in which famous generals are wont to appeal to the civil populace over the heads of civilian leaders. The military have two particularly good cards to play in this respect. First, modern wars tend to be fought by conscripts, and even though there are cultural and economic inequities in the working of the system, the fact of war *is* brought home to a broad segment of the populace. Once conscripts have been killed in large numbers, there is a very strong incentive to push the war on to total victory, for anything less will seem a needless sacrifice of life. That is, our "debt to the fallen," our "sacred compact with the dead," can be parlayed into a demand for escalation so that their "sacrifice will not have been in vain." Second, in wartime vigorous and radical action on the part of the military is likely to be more appealing to the mass of the population than restraint. Indeed, it is safe to say that most of the inhabitants of the Western democracies probably share their general's concept of victory.

At any rate, it has been difficult to "sell" the American public the idea of limited war—limited either in scope or in means.

What this all means is that we are currently faced with an ongoing dispute about how wars ought to be conducted. The dispute operates on many levels and often surfaces in the most peculiar ways and in the most peculiar places. The lines are not precisely drawn between the military and their civilian masters, but they are roughly so drawn. The military are too much imbued with the Clausewitzian conception of absolute war. Some, at least, of their scenarios are doubtless merely contingency planning: if we have nuclear weapons, for example, then we must at least plan for their possible use. But there are too many other cases in which the military aim for total military victory and argue tenaciously against any other possibility. The dreary story of the endless escalations in the Vietnam War ("Just give us another fifty thousand men and we can achieve victory") is eloquent testimony to that syndrome. There is, I believe, a practical moral imperative entailed by the present situation. When Clemenceau uttered his now famous truism, "War is too important a matter to be left to the generals," he meant that politicians ought to have a greater role in war planning and prosecution, but after the spectacle of five American presidents, each unable to wind up the war for fear of being "the first American president to lose a war," one is not comforted. Perhaps we ought to add to Clemenceau's remark, ". . . and to the politicians." The imperative would then be for the general public to become immersed in the study of war as a means of countering the elitism of civil and military strategists. I do not want to harp on the Vietnam conflict, but it is instructive to note that it was concluded under pressure of an aroused public, aroused finally by intellectuals and journalists. The recognition that what we were doing in Vietnam was both deeply immoral and strategically counterproductive was a conclusion to which politicians and generals were only very reluctantly brought.

Whether it is demonstrated by a famous civilian leader such as Senator Goldwater ("We ought to flatten Viet-nam and pave it over") or by a distinguished Air Force general such as Curtis Le May ("We ought to bomb them back into the Stone Age"), the futility of detaching war from political aims is obvious. Once political aims become the guiding force in the use of violence, then, inevitably, we begin to think beyond the battlefield to the shape of things after the fighting, of what sort of world we want to live in as a result of our decision to go to war. We will also be brought, I think, for prudential reasons to reflect upon the way our conduct of hostilities will be perceived by other nations (including our enemies). And we will adopt a *flexible* stance with respect to escalation as well as a willingness to maintain a degree of diplomatic contact. In other words, to adopt the viewpoint of political realism will be to find ourselves asking the kinds of questions raised by the doctrine of the just war. Political realism, so understood, and *bellum justum* are different sides of the same coin.*

*I am *not* saying that state interest and morality are strictly identical. Rather, when rulers begin to think about statecraft in terms of their long-range interests (with respect to war and peace) they will inevitably articulate these interests using a set of questions like those which make up the doctrine of the just war. This is a prudent move for states to make because a world where international relations were not so governed would (particularly in the modern era) contain extreme *danger*. This is perhaps the chief difference between the problem of war and other moral problems—while it might be imprudent in other areas of life to act from immediate self-interest rather than moral considerations, it is rarely positively dangerous to do so; one rarely risks life and limb by failing to be moral. But to "short-cut" the rules of war will probably risk precisely that, if not immediately, then in the long run.

Chapter 5

The Future of War

HAS WAR A FUTURE? It has been one of the main burdens of this work to establish, first, that in principle, there are conditions under which a moral agent could consent to the use of force and, second, that a refusal to use force under certain conditions would result in injustice. This moral claim is, I have contended, complementary to a realistic theory of statecraft. While this position has been reasonably satisfactory in the past, there is a widespread uneasiness that somehow the future will be very different from the past.

Part of the reason for the current concern about international violence is that we live in a peculiarly violent era; perhaps the closest historical parallel to our present position is Europe at the close of the Thirty Years' War. Interestingly, the excesses of that conflict brought about a revitalization of the rules of war which lasted until World War II. Now, of course, the potential for devastation posed by modern weapons is far greater than at any previous time. Under these circumstances many people have doubted whether we can go on doing "business as usual" without disastrous consequences.

Clausewitz argued that war carries within itself an impulse toward the absolute extreme: an instantaneous blow without duration. This was the ideal; in the real world "friction" and the political object would always render absolute war impossible. What Clausewitz could not foresee was that his definition of absolute war is a perfect description of a massive nuclear exchange. It is now practically possible to mobilize the entire power of the state in one instantaneous explosion resulting in total destruction. "Friction" is eliminated — the ideal is no longer modified by the real.

In earlier times, the hand of policy was at least partly effective as a restraint upon war because the means for doing violence were limited. This is, obviously, no longer the case. The crucial issue of our time is the increasing tension between the political object of war in the traditional sense and the possession of means which are wholly disproportionate to any conceivable political purpose. In the Preface to this work I suggested that weaponry alone cannot account for the peculiar horror of war in the modern world, that people must be psychologically "open" to its use. Unfortunately, because of the precedents set in World War II most nations *have* become quite fatalistic about this matter (as well as about terrorism in many other forms). We are now prepared to accept direct attacks upon noncombatant centers on a scale which would have appalled the civilized world of one hundred years ago. Certainly, there is also an acute awareness of the danger of war in our time. Greater efforts are being made to restrain and abolish war than in any previous era. But the "tyranny of means" is still with us.

The attempt to carry on with "business as usual" in the face of the possibility of total destruction by nuclear weapons is seen nowhere more clearly than in the strange world of the nuclear strategist. The curious fantasy world of these "Neo-Clausewitzians" (misleadingly so called) is beautifully captured in a remark by Anatol Rappaport:

Today speculations about "progress in the art of war" are carried on in a surrealistic mode, as witnessed by the situation described by Herman Kahn as "bizarre." In fact, not only is the depicted situation bizarre but also the setting in which the discussion of it takes place; a group of "college students, businessmen, members of the League of Women Voters, etc." arguing whether the "elimination" of Moscow or of Leningrad plus Kiev is the more "appropriate" response to the "elimination" of New York. I suspect that these discussions are possible only if one seals off from one's consciousness every shred of identification with the human race. This is not hard to do, if one is spared, as are the strategists and their receptive audiences, direct contact with the realities behind the fantasies.

This is why the Neo-Clausewitzians cannot be seen as sinister figures but only as bizarre ones. In the name of realism they perpetuate an obsolete collective state of mind which has brought humanity to the brink of disaster. What is unfolding is not a tragedy but a ghastly farce.[1]

Many people have, of course, argued that a kind of peace has been maintained by the threat of nuclear war and that this is a "positive" result. If I may employ an analogy, this "peace" is the peace of the airplane hijacker. By threatening to destroy the passengers and himself he imposes a kind of order upon the situation, but in doing so the passengers are held hostage and are dependent upon the mercies of their captors. When this fails they are doomed. Ecologists and other writers on survival have fancifully described our planet as "spaceship Earth." If one is permitted to speak in this way, then we may say that the passengers on this ship are currently being held as hostages and are subject to the whims and tender mercies of their "captors." The instability of this situation plus the immorality of coercion on such a vast scale make this situation profoundly immoral and dangerously imprudent. This being the case, it is hard to conceive of war of this type (if it can be called war at all) having a future.

What then of the future of conventional war and of insurgency? First of all, I do not believe that there is any strong evidence that the "balance of terror" has had a significant effect in preventing or even forestalling conventional war. The nuclear strategist's choice between, on the one hand, nuclear weapons and peace or, on the other, nuclear disarmament and vast conventional wars, is overstated. Conventional wars are undertaken, rather, only when they are conceived to be in the interests of states party to a conflict. Wars are *not* automatically induced by conditions of dispute or disagreement. They are based upon a highly complicated set of calculations about interests and consequences. The attempt to understand war as merely an expanded version of two individuals slugging it out in a barroom brawl is dangerously simplistic, and yet social scientists and others have consistently approached war in this way. Having done this, it then appears "obvious" to them that the possession of overwhelming power will necessarily be decisive. In fact, the only thing which nuclear weapons have obviously deterred is other nuclear weapons. If anything has been changed by the existence of nuclear weapons, it is that the major powers have tended to become less able to defend themselves through allowing their conventional arms to run down, assuming that any war would be a nuclear war. Conventional wars have not, I repeat, been in any way impeded by the existence of nuclear weapons. The actual impact of the atomic bomb upon modern history is summed up by John Lukacs:

In the wake of the two atomic bombs came a wave of mental shock. The public thinkers spoke up. From now on there were only two alternatives, they said; the United Nations or the Third World War, world government or the end of the world. They were wrong. In 1945 the dropping of the two atomic bombs on two cities in Japan was a great and monstrous event. Yet its consequences were overrated, both in the short and in the long run. In the short run, as we have seen, the atomic bomb was not the cause of Japan's surrender, since the Japanese government had been willing to negotiate some kind of an honorable capitulation months before the event of Hiroshima. In the long run the existence of atomic weapons changed the consequent world order (or disorder) surprisingly little. The possession of atomic or hydrogen bombs made the great states of the world less powerful, not more. For the first four years of the so-called Atomic Age the United States had a monopoly of the atomic bomb. This did not change the course of events a whit, since the United States had not the slightest inclination to use the atomic bomb in order to rectify the division of Europe or to rescue China from Communism. Fifteen years after 1945 the United States had enough atomic and hydrogen bombs to blow up most of the world; yet its government felt compelled to tolerate the establishment of a self-styled Communist dictatorship in Cuba, of all places. Ten years after 1945 Britain, fifteen years after 1945 France had their atomic and hydrogen bombs. The decline of their power was even more precipitous than before. Of course, we do not know what might happen if Levantine terrorists or petty tyrants get hold of atomic bombs. What we know — or, rather, what we ought to know — is that the atomic bomb, as Bernanos put it instantly in 1945, was a "triumph of technique over reason." And when technique triumphs over reason, human progress slows down instead of accelerating, and the result is a long and protracted kind of stagnation.[2]

But there is another kind of argument that has come to the fore in recent years which concentrates upon the psychological effect of battle on young men of the "modern" era. There are many versions of it, usually written by liberal psychologists and historians, but the most perceptive and extensive statement is found in John Keegan's book *The Face of Battle*. I cannot do complete justice to his argument without reproducing it fully; thus in what follows I shall try to paraphrase it and intersperse my comments.

Warfare, Keegan argues correctly, has become increasingly inhumane since the Middle Ages. During the Middle Ages single combat between gentlemen of more or less equal skill was thought to be the ideal instance of battle, both morally and professionally. With the invention of gunpowder and other weapons, the supremacy of single combat began to wane. The code of knightly conduct, however, continued as a practice long after single combats had been superseded:

The passion for single combat had kept it alive none the less and in so doing had held in check many of those innovations and inventions which were, when unleashed, to make Renaissance and post-Renaissance battles yet more costly than those of chivalry had been. Morally, therefore, the late medieval resistance of the gently born to military change had exerted a beneficial restraint. The echoes of the rear guard action they fought can be heard sounding through the din of the battles of the gunpowder age. And they reverberate still.[3]

"Gently born" echoes the "genteel arguments" objection of Margolis. One cannot, I believe, make too much of this attitude in trying to understand modern critics of *bellum justum*. It is certainly accurate to say that if one were casting about for a mode of fighting which would be most likely to conform to the various prohibitions and restraints which are part of the doctrine then single combat with weapons such as the sword or lance would probably be the best choice. That is, single combat with weapons of discrimination would mark the ideal limit of the doctrine. A spectrum might be conceived running from single combat on the one end to terrorism on the other. This would mark the limits on both ends of the doctrine. One must not, however, suppose that *any* deviation from single combats renders warfare immoral. The doctrine does seem to carry with it an imperative to "push" always in the direction of the single combat end of the spectrum rather than toward terrorism, but the disappearance of the ideal type of combat does not render *bellum justum* "otherworldly." We are still required to think about violence, at any level, in terms of the doctrine; but we must not be trapped into thinking that the view is useless or that it itself entails the abolition of war unless some ideal conditions can be realized. That would be like saying that unless men are perfectly moral, books on moral philosophy are all "otherworldly." Of course, some people have said this, but I think it is obvious which position is "otherworldly."

Keegan continues his argument by asserting that modern warfare "has increasingly become an intolerable experience for the majority (of modern conscripts who have to fight them). What has been happening is perhaps best described as an exaggerated social and cultural divergence from normality. Battle is always an abnormality.[4]

"Battle is always an abnormality." What kind of statement is this? If it is a factual claim about human nature or history, it is surely false. Studies of this matter have consistently shown that the human race has divided its time fairly equally between peace and war. One might as well generalize that peace is an abnormality. Is it, then, a moral judgment? War is certainly always an evil, but it is sometimes the lesser of evils. Yet, if the claim is being made that war is an absolute evil, then peace must be recognized as evil also, for "peace" is normally brought into being and maintained by force or threat of force. Moreover, the economic and cultural advantages which many nations now enjoy (notably the United States) were won in war. So battle is not in either of these two senses "abnormal." What is it then which makes our time unique? Keegan suggests three factors. The first is impersonality. Modern warfare, involving as it does mass armies, reduces the soldier to the status of a tiny cog in a gigantic machine. The term "cannon fodder" sums up this development. This occurs at a time when the peoples of the world are, in other areas of their lives, demanding an end to impersonality.

The second factor is deliberate cruelty. Although admitting that the modern era has seen the definition of the rules of war by the Hague and Geneva Conventions, Keegan thinks that these restraints have been negated by the development of weapons which are essentially indiscriminate. This occurs at a time when the peoples of the world are insisting that more humane treatment be the rule in other areas of life, for example, universal medical and social welfare, the abolition of capital punishment, and so on. The third element is coercion:

It is a function of the impersonality of modern war that the soldier is coerced, certainly at times by people he can identify, but more frequently, more continuously and more harshly by vast, unlocalized forces against which he may rail, but at which he cannot strike back and to which he must ultimately submit: The fire which nails him to the ground or drives him beneath it, the great distance which yawns between him and safety, the onward progression of a vehicular advance or retreat which carries him with it willy-nilly. The dynamic of modern battle impels more effectively than any system of discipline of which Frederick the Great could have dreamt.[5]

Coercion on such a scale is happening at a time when

the peoples of the world are increasingly demanding individual autonomy. Thus the conclusion is inescapable: "Impersonality, coercion, deliberate cruelty, all deployed on a rising scale, make the fitness of modern man to sustain the stress of battle increasingly doubtful":

The young have already made their decision. They are increasingly unwilling to serve as conscripts in armies they see as ornamental. The militant young have taken that decision a stage further: They will fight for the causes which they profess not through the mechanisms of the state and its armed power but, where necessary, against them, by clandestine and guerrilla methods. It remains for armies to admit that the battles of the future will be fought in never-never land. While the great armored hosts face each other across the boundary between east and west, no soldier on either side will concede that he does not believe in the function for which he plans and trains. As long as states put weapons in their hands, they will show each other the iron face of war. But the suspicion grows that battle has already abolished itself.[6]

Keegan, it seems to me, has got the cart squarely before the horse. It is not the incompatibility of the ideals of popular sovereignty with war which will cause war to eliminate itself. Rather, it is precisely those ideals which have made modern war possible, as I noted in the Preface to this work. For in the modern world these ideals can *only* be established within and effected by the political state. The "goods" of modern man are essentially *political* goods and, thus, the incentive to defend the state is greater than ever. It ought to be recalled that the youth of the 1930s were even more pacific than those of today. The conscription of Frederick the Great was not the conscription of the French Revolution. No amount of external coercion could have produced the mass battles of the post-cabinet wars. They occurred because enormous numbers of people were, and still are, willing to be so "coerced, impersonalized, and cruel." The doctrine of popular sovereignty can lead to no other result; or perhaps more mildly, this doctrine provides us with the real possibility of fighting unrestrained wars.

That being the case, we are not justified in supposing that war will abolish itself.

What all of this means is that if mankind is to survive, we must undertake the difficult intellectual work of thinking about how to *restrain* war. On the one hand, war is not going to go away, and on the other, it would be madness to abandon ourselves to the "Neo-Clausewitzians." I repeat, the way of salvation in this matter is to achieve a nexus of morality and prudence. *Bellum justum* does precisely that.

Appendix

On Guerrilla War

From B. H. Liddell-Hart, *Strategy: The Indirect Approach*, pages 379-82*

IN THE PAST, guerrilla war has been a weapon of the weaker side, and thus primarily defensive, but in the atomic age it may be increasingly developed as a form of aggression suited to exploit the nuclear stalemate. Thus the concept of "cold war" is now out of date, and should be superseded by that of "camouflaged war."

This broad conclusion, however, leads to a far-reaching and deeper question. It would be wise for the statesmen and strategists of the Western world to "learn from history" and avoid the mistakes of the past when seeking to develop a counter strategy in this kind of warfare.

The vast extension of such warfare during the last twenty years has, to a large extent, been the product of the war policy of instigating and fomenting popular revolt in enemy occupied countries that Britain, under Churchill's leadership, adopted in 1940 as a counter to the Germans—a policy subsequently extended to the Far East as a counter to the Japanese.

The policy was adopted with great enthusiasm and little question. Once the German tide of conquest had spread over most of Europe, it seemed the obvious course to pursue in the effort to loosen Hitler's grip. It was just the sort of thing that appealed to Churchill's mind and temperament. Besides his instinctive pugnacity and complete intentness on beating Hitler—regardless of what might happen afterward—he had been a close associate and admirer

*Reprinted by permission of Praeger Publishers, a division of Holt, Rinehart & Winston/CBS, New York. Copyright © 1954.

of Lawrence. He now saw the chance to practice on a large scale in Europe what the latter had demonstrated in a relatively limited part of the Arab zone.

To question the desirability of such a policy was to appear lacking in resolution and almost unpatriotic. Few dared to risk such an imputation, even if they doubted the ultimate effects of the policy on the recovery of Europe. War is always a matter of doing evil in the hope that good may come of it, and it is very difficult to show discrimination without failing in determination. Moreover the cautious line is usually a mistake in battle, where it is too commonly followed, so that it rarely receives credit on the higher plane of war policy, where it is more often wise but usually unpopular. In the fever of war, public opinion craves for the most drastic measures, regardless of where they may lead.

What were the results? The armed resistance forces undoubtedly imposed a considerable strain on the Germans. In Western Europe, the strain was most marked in France. They also proved a serious menace to the German communications in Eastern Europe and the Balkans. The best tribute to their effect comes from the evidence of the German commanders. Like the British commanders in Ireland during the "troubles," they were conscious of the worry and burden of coping with guerrilla foes who struck out of the blue and were shielded by the population.

At other times they were less effective than widespread passive resistance, and brought far more harm to the people of their own country. They provoked reprisals much more severe than the injury inflicted on the enemy. They afforded his troops the opportunity for violent action that is always a relief to the nerves of a garrison in an unfriendly country. The material damage that the guerrillas produced directly, and indirectly in the course of reprisals, caused much suffering among their own people and ultimately became a handicap to recovery after liberation.

But the heaviest handicap of all, and the most lasting one, was of a moral kind. The armed resistance movement attracted many "bad hats." It gave them license to indulge their vices and work off their grudges under the cloak of patriotism, thus giving fresh point to Dr. Johnson's remark that "patriotism is the last refuge of a scoundrel." Worse still was its wider effect on the younger generation as a whole. It taught them to defy authority and to break the rules of civic morality in the fight against the occupying forces. This left a disrespect for "law and order" that inevitably continued after the invaders had gone.

Violence takes much deeper root in irregular warfare than it does in regular warfare. In the latter it is counter-acted by obedience to constituted authority, whereas the former makes a virtue of defying authority and violating rules. It becomes very difficult to rebuild a country, and a stable state, on a foundation undermined by such experience.

A realization of the dangerous aftermath of guerrilla warfare came to me in reflection on Lawrence's campaigns in Arabia and in our discussion on the subject. My book on those campaigns, an exposition of the theory of guerrilla warfare, was taken as a guide by numerous leaders of commando units and resistance movements in the last war. Wingate, then only a captain serving in Palestine, came to see me shortly before it started and was obviously filled with the idea of giving the theory a fresh and wider application. But I was beginning to have doubts—not of its immediate efficacy, but of its long term effects. It seemed that they could be traced, like a thread, running through the persisting troubles that we, as the Turk's successors, were suffering in the same area where Lawrence had spread the Arab Revolt.

These doubts were deepened when re-examining the military history of the Peninsular War a century earlier and reflecting on the subsequent history of Spain. In that war, Napoleon's defeat of the Spanish regular armies was counter-balanced by the success of the guerrilla bands that replaced them. As a popular uprising against a foreign conqueror, it was one of the most effective on record. It did more than Wellington's victories to loosen Napoleon's grip on Spain and undermine his power. But it did not bring peace to liberated Spain, for it was followed by an epidemic of armed revolutions that continued in quick succession for half a century, and broke out again in this century.

Another ominous example was the way that the *franc-tireurs* created in France to harass the German invaders of 1870 had turned into a boomerang. They had been merely a nuisance to the invaders, but they had developed into the agency of the appalling fratricidal struggle known as the Commune. Moreover, the legacy of "illegitimate" action has been a continuing source of weakness in the subsequent history of France.

These lessons of history were too lightly disregarded by those who planned to promote violent insurrections as part of our war policy. The repercussions have had a shattering effect in the postwar years on the peace policy of the Western Alliance—and not only in providing both equipment and stimulus to anti-Western movements in Asia and Africa. For it early became apparent in the case of France that the military might of the Maquis as an instrument against the Germans was outweighed by the political and moral ill effects on the future. The disease has continued to spread. In conjunction with an unrealistic view and treatment of external troubles, it has undermined the stability of France and thereby dangerously weakened the position of NATO.

It is not too late to learn from the experience of history. However tempting the idea may seem of replying to our opponent's "camouflaged" war activities by counter-offensive moves of the same kind, it would be wiser to devise and pursue a more subtle and far-reaching counter-strategy. In any case, those who frame policy and apply it need a better understanding of the subject than has been shown in the past.

Notes

PREFACE

1. R. Leckie, *Warfare*, p. 17.

INTRODUCTION

1. R. Tucker, *The Just War*, p. 12.

2. J. Eppstein, *The Catholic Tradition of the Law of Nations.* There are many excellent studies of early Christian attitudes toward war and peace, but this one has the decided advantage of also containing all of the relevant documents, many of which are very difficult to locate otherwise. Generally speaking, Eppstein takes the view that Augustine's interpretations are very much in line with the teachings of Jesus and the beliefs of the early church. Without going into great historical detail (something I cannot do in the space of this work), I do not agree with Eppstein mainly because if he *is* right it becomes impossible to account for the time and space which Augustine (and others) devote to defending just-war theory. That is, Augustine is very much on the *defensive* in these writings, suggesting that he is arguing against the settled view to the contrary.

3. Leckie, *Warfare*, p. 19.

4. Eppstein, *The Catholic Tradition*, chap. 4. Other useful works are S. Ballie, *Prohibitions and Restraints in War* (New York: 1967); R. Bainton, *Christian Attitudes Toward War and Peace.*

CHAPTER 1

1. M. Walzer, *Just and Unjust Wars* (New York: Basic Books, 1973), p. 53.

147

2. J. Murray, *Morality and Modern War* (New York: Council on Religion and International Policy, 1970), p. 20.

CHAPTER 2

1. This is a modification of an example in A. MacIntyre, "The Idea of a Social Science," in *Against the Self-Images of the Age* (London: Duckworth, 1971), pp. 211-29.

2. There are many excellent discussions of the problem of prisoner immunity. The best is in M. Ramsey, *The Just War*.

3. J. Toland, *The Rising Sun* (New York: Random House, 1971), p. 218.

4. Toland, *Rising Sun*, chap. 4.

5. L. Forrester, *Fly for your Life*, pp. 301-303.

6. Ibid., p. 303.

7. L. Deighton, *Fighter* (New York: Knopf, 1977), p. 155.

8. E. Anscombe, "War and Murder," in *Nuclear Weapons and the Christian Conscience* (London: Stein & Day, 1962), p. 57.

9. R. Roberts, *War in the Air* (New York: Praeger, 1970), p. 342.

10. Ibid., pp. 242-48.

11. B. H. Liddell-Hart, *A History of the Second World War* (London: Cassell, 1970), p. 590.

12. Ibid., p. 594.

13. Ibid., p. 595.

14. Ibid., p. 596.

15. Ibid., p. 602.

16. Ibid., p. 605.

17. Ibid., p. 609.

18. Ibid.

19. M. Walzer, "World War II: Why Was This War Different?" in N. Cohen, ed., *War and Moral Responsibility* (Princeton, N.J.: Princeton University Press, 1974), p. 95.

20. J. Margolis, *Negativities* (Columbus, Ohio: Merrill, 1975), p. 53.

21. J. Finnis, *Natural Law and Natural Rights* (Oxford: Oxford University Press, 1979), p. 121. It is impossible in a book on applied ethics to do more than provide the bare outlines of an ethical theory. Interested readers should consult Finnis's book for further study.

22. A. Ryan, "Review of Jan Narveson's *Morality and Utility,*" *Philosophical Books* 9, no. 3.14.

23. Finnis, *Natural Law*, p. 117.

CHAPTER 3

1. R. Aron, *On War*, p. 86.
2. Ramsey, *The Just War*, p. 138.
3. *Time* Magazine, April, 1970, p. 32.
4. Taber, *The War of the Flea* (New York: Lyle Stuart, 1969), p. 131.
5. W. Laqueur, *Terrorism*, p. 119.
6. Thompson, *Defeating Communist Insurgency* (New York: Praeger, 1966), p. 224.
7. J. Larteguy, *The War in Vietnam* (London: Hutchinson, 1971), p. 89.
8. Sun Tzu, *The Art of War* (Oxford: Oxford University Press, 1963).
9. R. Asprey, *War in the Shadows* (Garden City, New York, 1975), p. 952.

CHAPTER 4

1. J. Narveson, "Pacifism: A Philosophical Analysis," in J. Rachels, *Moral Problems* (New York: Harper, 1979), pp. 346–471.
2. Ibid., p. 355.
3. Ibid., p. 359.
4. Narveson, unpublished paper, 1974.
5. G. Zahn, *An Alternative to War*, p. 18.
6. Ibid., p. 26.
7. Ibid., p. 73.
8. Anscombe, "War and Murder," in Rachels, *Moral Problems*, p. 293.
9. Zahn, *Alternative*, p. 56.
10. Ibid., p. 56.
11. Zahn, *Alternative*, p. 57.
12. The concept of the "Nation in Arms," which was the premise of conscription, made possible a radical alteration in tactics. With a seemingly inexhaustible supply of manpower, the French were prepared to adopt aggressive tactics—loss of life on the battlefield became less and less important as these could always be replaced by the engine of conscription. These developments culminated in Bonaparte's conception of battle as a violent clash of arms aimed at the destruction of the enemy army. Bonaparte's profligacy eventually turned the French against conscription, but initially it was the key to his success.

13. Rawls, *A Theory of Justice* (Oxford: Oxford University Press, 1972), p. 246.
14. Ramsey, *The Just War,* p. 92.
15. Rawls, *Justice,* p. 247.
16. Liddell-Hart, *Strategy,* p. 286.
17. V. Clausewitz, *On War,* p. 102.
18. Ibid., p. 103.
19. Ibid.
20. Liddell-Hart, *Strategy,* p. 288.
21. Clausewitz, *On War,* p. 107.
22. Ibid., p. 118.
23. Ibid., p. 401.
24. Ibid., p. 402.
25. B. Brodie, *War and Politics,* p. 376.
26. Ibid., p. 136.

CHAPTER 5

1. A. Rappaport, ed., Introduction, Clausewitz, *On War,* p. 80.
2. J. Lukacs, *1945: Year Zero* (New York: Macmillan), p. 138.
3. J. Keegan, *The Face of Battle* (Middlesex: Penguin, 1980), p. 317.
4. Ibid., p. 317.
5. Ibid., p. 324.
6. Ibid., p. 336.

Select Bibliography

Adcock, F. *Greek and Macedonian Art of War.* Berkeley: University of California Press, 1957.
———. *The Roman Art of War Under the Republic.* New York: Barnes and Noble, 1963.
Amrine, M. *The Great Decision: The Secret History of the Atomic Bomb.* New York: Putnam, 1959.
Andrzejewski, S. *Military Organization and Society.* London: Routledge and Kegan Paul, 1954.
Angell, N. *The Great Illusion.* New York: Putnam's, 1911.
Aron, R. *The Century of Total War.* Boston: Beacon, 1955.
———. *On War.* Garden City, N.Y.: Norton, 1968.
———. *Peace and War.* London: Weidenfeld and Nicolson, 1967.
———. *War and Industrial Society.* New York: Oxford University Press, 1958.
Bainton, R. *Christian Attitudes to War and Peace.* New York: Macmillan, 1973.
Ballou, A. *Christian Non-Resistance.* New York: Da Capo Press, 1970.
Barnett, C. *The Swordbearers: Supreme Command in the First World War.* New York: Morrow, 1964.
Batchelder, R. *The Irreversible Decision: 1939-1950.* New York: 1965.
Bennet, J. *Nuclear Weapons and the Conflict of Conscience.* New York: Scribner, 1962.
———. *Moral Tensions in International Affairs.* New York: Council on Religion and International Policy, 1970.
Bloch, I. *The Future of War.* Boston: Ginn, 1902.
Boyle, A. *Trenchard.* London: Collins, 1962.
Brodie, B. *A Guide to Naval Strategy.* New York: Praeger, 1968.
———. *Morals and Strategy.* Santa Monica, Ca.: Rand Corporation, 1964.

————. *Strategic Air Power in World War II.* Santa Monica, Ca.: Rand Corporation, 1957.

————. *Strategy in the Missile Age.* Princeton, N.J.: Princeton University Press, 1959.

————. *War and Politics.* New York: Macmillan, 1973.

————, and F. Brodie. *From Cross-Bow to H-Bomb.* New York: Dell, 1962.

Buccheim, L. G. *U-Boat War.* New York: Knopf, 1978.

Buchan, A. *War in Modern Society.* London: Watts, 1966.

Burne, A. H. *The Art of War on Land.* Harrisburg, Pa.: Stackpole, 1966.

————. *Persia and the Greeks: The Defense of the West, 546-478 B.C.* New York: St. Martin's, 1962.

Bury, J. *A History of Greece.* London: Macmillan, 1959.

Carman, W. *A History of Firearms from Earliest Times to 1914.* New York: St. Martin's, 1956.

Chandler, D. *The Campaigns of Napoleon.* New York: Macmillan, 1966.

Clarkson, A., and T. Cochrane. *War as a Social Institution: The Historian's Perspective.* New York: Columbia University Press, 1941.

Clausewitz, V. *On War.* Middlesex: Penguin, 1976.

Cohen, M., T. Nagel, and T. Scanlon. *War and Moral Responsibility.* Princeton, N.J.: Princeton University Press, 1974.

Davies, G. *Wellington and His Army.* Oxford: Oxford University Press, 1954.

Dickens, G. *Bombing and Strategy.* London: S. Low, 1947.

DuPicq, A. *Battle Studies.* Harrisburg, Pa.: Military Service, 1947.

Earle, E. M. *Makers of Modern Strategy: Military Thought from Machiavelli to Hitler.* New York: Atheneum, 1966.

Ellis, J. *The Social History of the Machine Gun.* New York: Pantheon, 1975.

Erasmus. *Against War.* Boston: Merrymount, 1907.

Eppstein, J. *The Catholic Tradition of the Law of Nations, with Documents.* London: Burns & Oates, 1935.

Fall, B. *The Two Vietnams.* New York: Praeger, 1967.

Falls, Cyril. *The Art of War: From the Age of Napoleon to the Present Day.* London: Oxford University Press, 1961.

————. *The First World War.* London: Longmans, 1964.

————. *A Hundred Years of War.* New York: Collier, 1962.

Ferkis, V. *Foreign Aid: Moral and Political Aspects.* New York: Council on Religion and International Policy, 1970.

Finnis, John. *Natural Law and Natural Rights.* Oxford: Oxford University Press, 1979.

Forrester, L. *Fly for Your Life: The Story of R. R. Stanford Tuck, D.S.O., D.F.C., and Two Bars.* New York: Bantam, 1978.

Frederick II of Prussia. *Instructions for his Generals.* Harrisburg, Pa.: Stackpole, 1951.

Fredette, R. *The Sky on Fire: The First Battle of Britain, 1917-1918, and the Birth of the Royal Air Force.* New York: Holt, Rinehart, and Winston, 1966.

Fuller, J. *The Conduct of War, 1789-1961.* London: Eyre and Spottiswodde, 1961.
——. *War and Western Civilization: A Study of War as a Political Instrument and as an Expression of Mass Democracy.* London: Duckworth, 1932.

Gallois, P. *The Balance of Terror: Strategy for the Nuclear Age.* Boston: Houghton Mifflin, 1961.

Gaynor, F. *The New Military and Naval Directory.* New York: Philosophical Library, 1951.

Ginsberg, M. *The Critique of War.* Chicago: Henry Regenery, 1969.

Goerlitz, W. *History of the German General Staff, 1657-1945.* New York: Praeger, 1953.

Gray, G. *The Warriors.* New York: Harcourt, Brace, 1959.

Greenspan, M. *Soldiers' Guide to the Laws of War.* Washington, D.C.: Public Affairs Press, 1969.

Grotius. *De jure belli ac pacis.* The Hague: Nijhoff, 1948.

Halperen, M. *The Morality and Politics of Intervention.* New York: Council on Religion and International Policy, 1971.

Harris, A. *Bomber Offensive.* London: Collins, 1947.

Howard, M. *The Franco-Prussian War.* New York: Collier, 1969.
——. *Soldiers and Governments: Nine Studies in Civil-Military Relations.* Bloomington: Indiana University Press, 1957.
——. *War and the Liberal Conscience.* New Brunswick, N.J.: Rutgers University Press, 1978.

Huntington, S. *The Soldier and the State: The Theory and Politics of Civil-Military Relations.* Cambridge, Mass.: Harvard University Press, 1957.

James, W. "The Moral Equivalent of War." New York: AAIC,

1916.

Jomini, H. *Summary of the Art of War.* Harrisburg, Pa.: Stackpole, 1972.

Kahn, H. *On Escalation.* New York: Praeger, 1965.

———. *On Thermonuclear War.* Princeton, N.J.: Princeton University Press, 1960.

———. *Thinking About the Unthinkable.* New York: Avon, 1969.

Keegan, J. *The Face of Battle.* New York: Viking, 1976.

Keen, M. *The Law of War in the Late Middle Ages.* London: Routledge and Kegan Paul, 1965.

Knudson. *The Philosophy of War and Peace.* New York: Abingdon, 1947.

Kranzberg, R., and T. Purcell. *Technology in Western Civilization.* New York: Oxford University Press, 1967.

Laquer, W. *Guerrilla.* Boston: Little, Brown, 1977.

———. *Terrorism.* Boston: Little, Brown, 1977.

Leckie, R. *Warfare.* New York: Harper and Row, 1970.

Lewis, J. *The Case Against Pacifism.* New York: Garland, 1973.

Liddell-Hart, B. H. *Strategy: The Indirect Approach.* New York: Praeger, 1954.

Luvass, J. *Frederick the Great on the Art of War.* New York: Free Press, 1966.

Machiavelli, N. *The Art of War.* Indianapolis: Bobbs-Merrill, 1965.

———. *The Prince.* Translated by L. Ricci. New York: Mentor, 1952.

Mahan, A. *The Influence of Sea Power on History, 1660–1783.* New York: Hill and Wang, 1957.

Mao Tse-tung. *On Protracted War.* Peking: Foreign Language Press, 1954.

Millis, W. *Arms and the State: Civil-Military Elements in National Policy.* New York: Twentieth-Century Fund, 1958.

Montgomery, B. L. *A History of Warfare.* London: Collins, 1968.

Mumford, L. *Technics and Civilization.* New York: Harcourt, Brace, 1934.

Nef, J. *War and Human Progress.* Cambridge, Mass.: Harvard University Press, 1950.

Noel-Baker, P. *The Geneva Protocol.* London: P. S. King and Son, 1925.

O'Brien, W. *War and/or Survival.* Garden City, N.Y.: Doubleday, 1969.

Oman, C. *The Art of War in the Middle Ages.* New York: Burt Franklin, 1969.

Phillips, T. R. *Roots of Strategy.* Harrisburg, Pa.: Military Service, 1940.

Preston, R., and S. Wise. *Men in Arms.* New York: Praeger, 1962.

Pustay, J. *Counter Insurgency Warfare.* New York: Free Press, 1965.

Ramsey, P. *The Just War: Force and Political Responsibility.* New York: 1968.

———. *War and the Christian Conscience.* Durham, N.C.: Duke University Press, 1961.

Rappoport, A. *Strategy and Conscience.* New York: Harper and Row, 1964.

Ropp, T. *War in the Modern World.* New York: Macmillan, 1965.

Russell, B. *Why Men Fight.* New York: Century, 1917.

Sampson, R. *The Discovery of Peace.* New York: Pantheon, 1973.

Saxe, M. *Reveries on the Art of War.* Harrisburg, Pa.: Military Service, 1944.

Sellman, R. *Medieval English Warfare.* London: Roy, 1964.

Sheppard, P. *A Short History of the British Army.* London: Constable, 1950.

Shinn, R. *Wars and Rumors of Wars.* New York: Abingdon, 1972.

Shotwell, J. *Plans and Protocols to End War.* New York: 1925.

Sombart, W. *The Quintessence of Capitalism.* New York: Fertig, 1967.

Stein, W. *Nuclear Weapons: A Catholic Response.* New York: Sheed and Ward, 1961.

Strachey, A. *The Unconscious Motives of War: A Psychoanalytic Contribution.* New York: Hillary, 1957.

Stoessinger, C. *Why Nations Go to War.* New York: St. Martin's, 1974.

Taylor, E. *The Strategy of Terror.* Boston: Houghton Mifflin, 1940.

Taylor, T. *Nuremberg and Vietnam.* Chicago: Quadrangle, 1970.

Tolstoi, L. *The Kingdom of God.* London: Oxford University Press, 1936.

Toynbee, A. *War and Civilization.* New York: Oxford University Press, 1950.

Tucker, R. *The Just War: Exposition of the American Concept.*

Baltimore, Md.: Johns Hopkins University Press, 1960.

Turney-High, H. *Primitive War.* Columbia: University of South Carolina Press, 1949.

U.S. Military Academy. *Jomini, Clausewitz, and Schlieffen.* West Point, N.Y.: Government Printing Office, 1951.

Vagts, A. *A History of Militarism.* Glencoe, Ill.: Free Press, 1967.

Vegetius, F. *The Military Institutions of the Romans.* Harrisburg, Pa.: Military Service, 1944.

Vitoria, F. *De Indis et De jure belli.* Washington, D.C.: Carnegie Institute, 1917.

Webster, C., and N. Frankland. *The Strategic Air Offensive Against Germany, 1939-1945.* London: Her Majesty's Stationery Office, 1961.

Wedgwood, C. *The Thirty Years' War.* Harmondsworth: Penguin, 1961.

Wells, D. *The War Myth.* New York: Pegasus, 1967.

Wintringham, T. H. *Weapons and Tactics.* London: Faber and Faber, 1940.

Wise, S. "The Balance of Nuclear Terror," *Queen's Quarterly* 67 (1960).

Wright, Q. *A Study of War.* Chicago: Chicago University Press, 1965.

Zahn, G. *An Alternative to War.* New York: Council on Religion and International Policy, 1970.

Index

War and Justice,

designed by Bill Cason, was set in eleven-point Caledonia by the University of Oklahoma Press and printed offset on sixty-pound Warren's Old Style, a permanized sheet, by the University of Oklahoma Printing Services, with case binding by Ellis Bindery.